ent Chinese Economic Reports series provides insights into the economic
ent of one of the largest and fastest growing economies in the world;
idely discussed internationally, many facets of its current development
nknown to the English speaking world. All reports contain new data,
s previously unknown or unavailable outside of China. The series covers
development, industry reports, as well as special topics like environmental
graphical issues.

formation about this series at http://www.springer.com/series/11028

Current Chinese Economic Re

The Curr
developm
though v
remain u
which w
regional
or demo

More in

Center for Macroeconomic Research
of Xiamen University

China's Macroeconomic Outlook

Quarterly Forecast and Analysis Report, September 2016

Springer

Center for Macroeconomic Research
of Xiamen University
Xiamen, Fujian
China

Grants: the major projects of China National Social Science Foundation (15ZDC011, 13&ZD029), the major research projects of philosophy and social sciences of China's Ministry of Education of China (15JZD016, 14JZD011), the key research projects of the Key Research Institutions of Humanities and Social Sciences of China's Ministry of Education (14JJD790007, 13JJD790026, 13JJD790025), the general projects of China National Social Science Foundation (15BJL008), the youth projects of China National Social Science Foundation (13CJL017, 11CJY073), the youth project of China Natural Science Foundation (71503222).

ISSN 2194-7937 ISSN 2194-7945 (electronic)
Current Chinese Economic Report Series
ISBN 978-981-10-3279-0 ISBN 978-981-10-3280-6 (eBook)
DOI 10.1007/978-981-10-3280-6

Library of Congress Control Number: 2016959400

Printed on acid-free paper

This Springer imprint is published by Springer Nature
The registered company is Springer Nature Singapore Pte Ltd.
The registered company address is: 152 Beach Road, #22-06/08 Gateway East, Singapore 189721, Singapore

Preface

This report is a partial result of the China's Quarterly Macroeconometric Model (CQMM), a project developed and maintained by the Center for Macroeconomic Research (CMR) at Xiamen University. The CMR is one of the Key Research Institutes of Humanities and Social Sciences sponsored by the Ministry of Education of China, focuses on China's economic growth and macroeconomic policy. The CMR started to develop the CQMM for purpose of short-term forecasting, policy analysis and simulation in 2005.

Based on the CQMM, the CMR and its partners hold press conference to release forecast for China major macroeconomic variables. Since July, 2006, twenty quarterly reports on China's macroeconomic outlook have been presented and eleven annual reports have been published.

This 21st quarterly report was presented at the Forum on China's Macroeconomic Prospects and Press Conference of CQMM on September 2, 2016. This conference was jointly held by Xiamen University, Economic Information Daily at Xinhua News Agency, and the Australian National University.

Xiamen, China

Center for Macroeconomic Research
of Xiamen University

Acknowledgements

According to the Chinese Pinyin order of their names, the 116 experts who joined this questionnaire survey were: Bai Peiwen, Chang Xin, Chen Changbing, Chen Jianbao, Chen Kunting, Chen Langnan, Chen Lei, Chen Menggen, Chen Shoudong, Chen Xue Bin, Chen Yanbin, Chen Yongjun, Chen Zhiyong, Dai Kuizao, Deng Xiang, Fan Conglai, Gao Bo, Guo Xibao, Guo Xiaohe, Han Zhaozhou, He Jingtong, Huang Xianhai, Jin Tao, Jian Xinhua, Jiang Yongmu, Jin Xiangrong, Lai Desheng, Li Chunqi, Li Jianwei, Li Jun, Li Shi, Li Xuesong, Li Yingdong, Lin Xuegui, Liu Fengliang, Liu Jianping, Liu Jinquan, Liu Qiongzhi, Liu Shiguo, Liu Xiaoxin, Liu Yunzhong, Liu Zhibiao, Ma Ying, Pang Jingju, Pang Xiaobo, Qiu Chongming, Qiu Dong, Qu Wanwen, Ren Baoping, Ren Ruoen, Shao Yihang, Shen Kunrong, Shi gang, Shi Jinchuan, Su Jian, Sun Wei, Tang Jijun, Tian Ruzhu, Wang Changyun, Wang hongjun, Wang Tongsan, Wang Yida, Wang Cheng, Wang Dashu, Wang guocheng, Wang Haijie, Wang Jiping, Wang Jinzhao, Wang Liyong, Wang Luolin, Wang Meijin, Wang Xi, Wang Yongqin, Wang Yuesheng, Wen Chuanhao, Wu Xinru, Xiao Xingzhi, Xie Pan, Xu Yifan, Xu Wenbin, Xu Xianchun, Yang Ping, Yang Chengyu, Yang Chunxue, Yang Cuihong, Yang Ruilong, Yang Zhiyong, Ye Shisheng, Yi Xianrong, Yin Xingmin, Yu Li, Yu Zuo, Yuan Fuhua, Zang Xuheng, Zhang Donghui, Zhang Liqun, Zhang Liancheng, Zhang Long,Zhang Mingzhi, Zhang Monan, Zhang Ping, Zhang Yishan, Zhang Shuguang, Zhao Zhenquan, Zhao Zhijun, Zheng Chaoyu, Zheng Tingguo, Zhong Chunping, Zhou Liqun, Zhou Zejiong, Zhu Baohua, Zhu Jianping, Zhu Qigui, Zhuang Zongming.

The experts who joined this questionnaire survey are from institutions like the Fiscal Science Research Institute of the Ministry of Finance, Ministry of Finance Comprehensive Department, National Development and Reform Commission, China's National Bureau of Statistics, Macroeconomic Research Department of Development Research Center of the State Council, Social Development Research Department of Development Research Center of the State Council, Development Strategy and Regional Economic Research Department of Development Research Center of the State Council, The Ministry of Commerce, the China Center for international economic exchanges, National Academy of Economic Strategy of CASS, The Institute of Finance and Banking of CASS, The Institute of Economics of CASS, The Institute of World Economy and Politics of CASS, The Institute of Quantitative Economics and Technical Economics of Chinese Academy of Social Sciences, The Center for Research Forecast of CAS, Economic Information Daily, Unirule Institute of Economics, Taiwan Academia Sinica, Taiwan Chung-Hua Institution for Economic Research and universities like Anhui Finance and Economics University, Peking University, Beijing Normal University, Beihang University, Chongqing Technology and Business University, Dongbei University of Finance and Economics, Dongbei Normal University, University of International Business and Economics, Fudan University, Fujian Normal University, Henan University, Hunan University, East China Normal University, Huaqiao Universtity, Huazhong University of Science and Technology, Jilin University, Jinan University, Jiangxi University of Finance and Economics,Lanzhou University, Liaoning University, Nanchang university, Nanjing University, Nankai University, Tsinghua University, Shandong University, Shaanxi Normal University, Shanghai University of Finance and Economics, Shanghai University of International Business and Economics, Shanghai Jiao Tong University, Capital University of Economics and Business, Sichuan University, National Taiwan University, Tianjin University of Finance and Economics, Tianjin University of Commerce, Wuhan University, Xi'an Jiao Tong University, Northwest University, Southwestern University of Finance and Economics, Xiamen University, Zhejiang University, Zhejiang University of Finance and Economics, Zhejiang University of Technology, Zhengzhou University, Renmin University of China, Zhongnan University of Economics and Law, Sun Yat-Sen University, Central University of Finance and Economics, etc.

Thank for the active participation and insights of all the experts mentioned above sincerely.

Contents

1 China Economic Performance in the First Half of 2016 1
1.1 Structural Transformation Persisted and the Labor Market Stayed Robust 1
1.2 Total Investment Growth Edged Down While Private Investment Growth Dropped Dramatically 6
1.3 Consumption Growth Remained Steady Despite Household Income Growth Decelerated 10
1.4 Foreign Trade Growth Remained Sluggish 12
1.5 The CPI Sustained Stable While the Decline in PPI Slowed 14
1.6 Bank Credit Rose Rapidly While the Gap Between M1 and M2 Growth Widened 15
1.7 Fiscal Revenues Saw Fast Growth and Fiscal Expenditures Expanded Dramatically 17

2 Quarterly Forecast for 2016–17 23
2.1 Assumptions on Exogenous Variables 23
2.1.1 Growth Rates of the United States and the Euro Area 23
2.1.2 The Exchange Rates 23
2.1.3 Growth Rate of the Broad Money Supply (M2) 24
2.2 Quarterly Forecast for China Major Macroeconomic Indicators in 2016–17 26
2.2.1 GDP Growth Rates 26
2.2.2 Major Prices Indices 26
2.3 Growth Rates of Other Major Macroeconomic Indicators 28
2.3.1 Growth Rates of Exports, Imports, and Foreign Exchange Reserves 28
2.3.2 Growth Rates of Investment in Fixed Assets 30
2.3.3 Growth Rates of Consumption 31

3 Policy Simulation: Macroeconomic Effects of Slowdown in Private Investment Growth 35
3.1 Background 35
3.2 Further Research. 41
3.3 Policy Simulation 43
3.3.1 Model Specification Adjustment 43
3.3.2 Simulation Scenarios Planning 43
3.3.3 Simulation Results 44

4 Policy Implications and Suggestions. 51

Appendix: Report on the Questionnaire Survey on China's Macroeconomic Situation and Policy in 2016 55

Contributors

Principal Investigator

Li Wenpu Center for Macroeconomic Research of Xiamen University, Xiamen, China

Research Team Members

Min Gong, Zhiyuan Lin, Yu Liu, Shengrong Lu, Guifu Chen, Changlin Yu, Yanwu Wang, Jing Li, Huakun Wu

This report is contributed by Zhiyuan Lin, Jing Li, Yanwu Wang, and Changli Yu. It is revised by Wenpu Li, Min Gong, and Shengrong Lu. The raw data are processed by Huakun Wu.

Executive Summary

The first half of 2016 saw the continued slowdown of China's economic growth. The real GDP growth increased by 6.7%, down by 0.3 percentage points over the same period last year. Given the relatively steady growth of consumption and persistently subdued foreign trade, the deceleration of total investment growth was the key factor of economic slowdown. Due to measures to curb excess capacity, investment in mining dropped sharply, and manufacturing investment growth edged down. High corporate leverage and the decline in the returns on investment (ROI) weakened investment willingness among businesses. And the sharp drop of private investment growth reflects the lack of drivers of endogenous investment. For these reasons, the downward trend in total investment growth would not be offset by either the property investment growth supported by credit expansion or the accelerating infrastructure investment growth led by the government, or both. In the second half of 2016, total investment growth is expected to slow down further, and marginal effects of investment on economic growth would continue fading.

Since the global financial crises, due to the dramatic changes in the domestic and international economic environment, the previous investment-driven and export-oriented growth pattern has become unsustainable. Given sluggish external demand and increasing costs of production factors, it is urgent for China to change its current growth pattern. China's macroeconomic policy has to make a difficult tradeoff between near-term demand management measures and long-term supply-side structural transformation, while in the meantime addressing financial stability risks.

Nevertheless, during China's transition from a high-middle income country to a high-income country, the domestic demand structure is being updated, and the contribution of consumption to economic growth is rising. All these have brought about not only continuous expansion of the services industry, but constant adjustment of industrial structure to meet the transformation of demand structure. And the impact of decelerating economic growth on labor markets has been so far relatively small due to the continuous expansion of the services industry. Furthermore, measures to cut backward production capacity have come into force. Supported by various policies to reduce business cost burden, industrial production picked up slightly, and financial performance of enterprises began to improve. Manufacturing structure carries on continuous improvement, and its growth rate of profit restores stability. Transformation and upgrading of the industrial structure are accelerating, and the newly-emerging strategic industries grow rapidly. In the long run, the positive effects of structural transformation are going to be the fundamental forces to stabilize China's economic growth.

According to the China's Quarterly Macroeconometric Model (CQMM), China's economic growth is expected to continue edging down due to decelerating investment growth and week exports growth, while the deflation risks remain low.

1. The GDP growth in 2016 is projected to rise 6.63%, 0.3 percentage points higher than that over 2015. The CPI is expected to climb 2.01%, an increase of 0.57 percentage points over 2015. The PPI is forecast to drop by 3.19%, 2.01 percentage points higher than that in 2015. And the GDP deflator is projected to pick up by 0.79%, an increase of 1.2 percentage points over 2015.
2. The decline in growth of manufacturing investment and private investment has put pressures on total investment growth. The growth of investment in fixed assets (excluding rural households) in 2016 is projected to expand by 9.72%, a drop of 0.47 percentage points over 2015.
3. The growth of per capita real disposable income of households is expected to edge down, suggesting that the household consumption is expected to slow down. The total retail sales of consumer goods in 2016 are forecast to go up by 10.3%, a decline of 0.4 percentage points over 2015.
4. Both the result of UK referendum and the lower-than-expected US GDP growth rate in the second quarter imply that the materialization of an important downside risk for advanced economies. The total value of exports in dollar terms in 2016 is expected to fall by 6.01%, down by 3.79 percentage points over 2015. The total value of imports is projected to decline by 14.12%, slightly up by 0.27 percentage points over 2015.
5. Owing to RMB depreciation expectations arising from economic slowdown and pressures put by capital outflows, China is projected to continue depleting its foreign exchange reserves to stabilize RMB. Foreign exchange reserves at the end of 2016 would fall to 2.98 trillion dollars.

That the private investment growth dropped dramatically is one of the most significant macroeconomic events in 2016. Policy simulation in this report shows that if the ROI would be increased to about 8%, around which stayed in 2013, then the share of private investment would be raised significantly, and that would make China maintain its growth rate at about 7–8%. Conversely, if there would be a sharp fall of ROI, then the private investment would correspondingly drop dramatically, which would make China's economic growth rate drop below its present level. Thus, the results of policy simulation verify that China's economy cannot suffer a sharp fall in private investment growth, whatever in the near term or in the long term.

We also find that, owing to the global rebalancing and the domestic structural transformation, the private investment growth continued slowing down after 2011.

Nevertheless, the dramatic drop of its growth since early 2016 is largely attributable to China's current implementation of supply-side structural reform. Therefore, we suggest that, in the short run, the demand-side measures to stabilize economic growth should be continued in order to resume private entrepreneurs' expectations on China's economic outlook, while in the long run, institutional reforms needed by the supply-side structural reforms should be made.

The policy suggestions are presented as follows:

1. Implement neutral monetary policy to stabilize economic growth. The monetary policy in the second half of 2016 should return to be neutral, guiding the bank credit to enter into the real economy and help it recover, while in the meantime reining financial assets bubbles. Given that the external environment for China to reduce interest rates has been relieved, while the economic downside pressures are still strong, we suggest that the central bank cut interest rates and the reserve requirement ratios in the second half of 2016.
2. Carry out expansionary fiscal policy to lift China's economic growth. Given that the monetary policy returns to be neutral, the fiscal policy should play major role. On the expenditures side, infrastructure investment and expenditures on people's livelihood should be the focuses of fiscal expenditure policy. On the revenues side, in the near term, a feasible approach is to make some minor changes in current policies within the established framework of tax law.
3. Lower market entry barriers and stabilize business expectations for private investment. At the stage of demand structural transformation, the capital tends to exit from sunset industries and overcapacity sectors and then enter into sunrise industries and newly-emerging demand sectors. However, further development of the services industry is being stalled by commonly existing monopoly, regulation, and ownership discrimination. Thus, it is urgent for the government to clean up these barriers and encourage equal competitions. In the meantime, it is also necessary to open new investment fields, lower investment costs, and improve the ROI of private capital.
4. Take measures to support private financing. To address the long-standing problem that small and micro businesses are finding it difficult and costly to obtain financing, the government should take measures to help provide financial services to private businesses, provide credit consulting service and information service to private businesses, and establish medium and small financial institutions sponsored by private capital, and so on, in order to expand financing channels for private businesses. China's current financial institutions are mainly state-owned and monopolistic, determining that private businesses' financing problem is hard to solve. If freer, more open, and more competitive financial institutions can be established, then the information asymmetry problem between borrowers and lenders may be solved. And then, the problem of high financing cost faced by private businesses may be alleviated. In addition, multi-level capital markets should be established to open more convenient financing channels for private businesses.

5. Make reforms on taxation structure to relieve business tax burden. The cost reduction task, as one of measures in the context of the supply-side structural reform, should be taken on not only by the businesses through technological innovation and management improvement, but by the government through tax cuts and reduction in fees and charges. On its road to establish modern public finance, China should not only continue to clean up unnecessary and/or unreasonable charges and fees, but put more emphasis on changing its current tax system centered on the indirect tax to a new one centered on the direct tax as the main body. To be specific, the government should reduce the current VAT and consumption tax rates, try to levy possession property tax and estate and gift tax, and adopt comprehensive personal tax system, in order to reduce business tax burden and let these direct taxes perform their functions in income redistribution, and thus stimulate household consumption demand.

Chapter 1
China Economic Performance in the First Half of 2016

China's economic growth continued to slow down further. In the first half of 2016, real GDP growth[1] moderated to 6.7% YoY from 6.9% in 2015 and 7% a year earlier respectively. Of the industrial enterprises above designated size, value added decreased marginally to 6.0% from 6.1% in 2015 and 6.3% a year ago (see Fig. 1.1). China's continued economic slowdown reflects that, given subdued external demand, increasing labor cost, and end of property boom, the investment-driven and export-oriented growth model, which has served China well in the past, is now in a difficult position as returns on investment (ROI) has fallen.

As the structural transformation becomes more evident, China's growth will continue to slow down in the medium term. Due to overcapacity in manufacturing, overstock in real estate, and high corporate debt load, the total investment growth decelerated, typically, the private investment growth fell sharply. China's macroeconomic policy has to make a difficult tradeoff between near-term demand management measures and long-term supply-side structural transformation, while in the meantime addressing financial stability risks.

1.1 Structural Transformation Persisted and the Labor Market Stayed Robust

China's transition is undergoing its difficult stage while seeking new growth engines. With the changing demand structure and the accelerating supply-side structural reform, China's economic structure is being adjusted slowly. Consumption's contribution to GDP growth is rising, industrial structure is being upgraded gradually,

[1]In this report, all the variables/indicators are taken as nominal ones, that is, they are measured at current prices, unless they are clearly indicated as "real". All the growth rates are measured year-on-year (YoY), unless they are clearly indicated as "quarter-on-quarter (QoQ)".

Center for Macroeconomic Research of Xiamen University,
China's Macroeconomic Outlook, Current Chinese Economic
Report Series, DOI 10.1007/978-981-10-3280-6_1

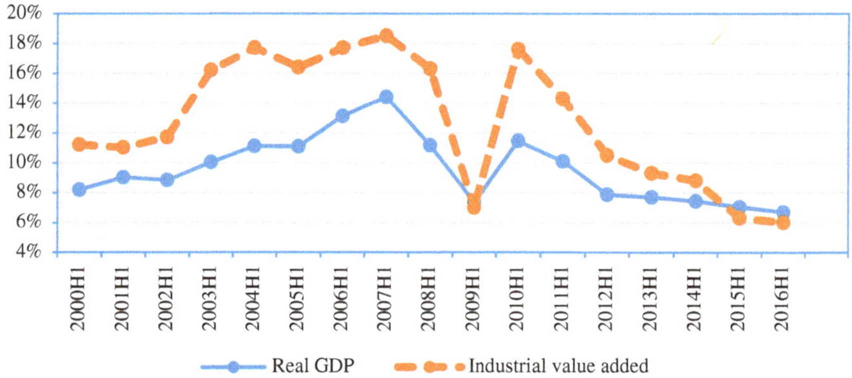

Fig. 1.1 GDP growth and industrial value added growth edged down YoY. *Source* CQMM team calculations on CEIC data

and the impact of decelerating economic growth on labor markets has been so far relatively small due to the continuous expansion of services industry.

First, given decelerating investment growth, the contribution of consumption to GDP growth rose rapidly. In the first half of 2016, total investment in fixed assets (FAI) grew by 9.0% YoY, 2.5 percentage points lower than that of the same period last year. Gross capital formation accounts for 37% of GDP growth, a decline of 0.6 percentage points over the same period last year. Though household income growth continues to edge down, consumption growth remains relatively stable. Total retail sales of consumer goods grew by 10.3%, 0.1 percentage points lower than that of the same period last year. Final consumption expenditure accounts for 73.4% of GDP growth, a drop of 13.2 percentage points over the same period last year (see Fig. 1.2).

Second, the tertiary industry keeps expanding and the industrial sector is being upgraded. Jointly supported by increasing household income and the shift of demand structure, the tertiary industry developed rapidly. In the first half of 2016, value added from the tertiary industry accounts for 54.1% of GPP, an increase of 1.8 percentage points over the same period last year, 14.7 percentage points higher than that in the secondary industry (see Fig. 1.3).

Thirdly, due to continuous expansion of the tertiary sector, which is working as the main force to absorb employment, moderating economic growth has not dragged down urban employment growth. At the end of the first and second quarter of 2016, the registered unemployment rates in urban areas are 4.04 and 4.05% respectively, staying at relatively low levels. Affected by the accelerating reform in curbing overcapacity this year, the number of unemployment insurance payments rose marginally to 2.31 million in the first quarter and 2.37 million in the second quarter, both up by 0.16 million YoY (see Fig. 1.4). Nevertheless, due to positive effects of structural adjustment, 7.17 million new urban jobs had been created in the first half of 2016, matching the level in the same period a year earlier. National requirement rates of jobs are 1.07 in the first quarter and 1.05 in the second quarter,

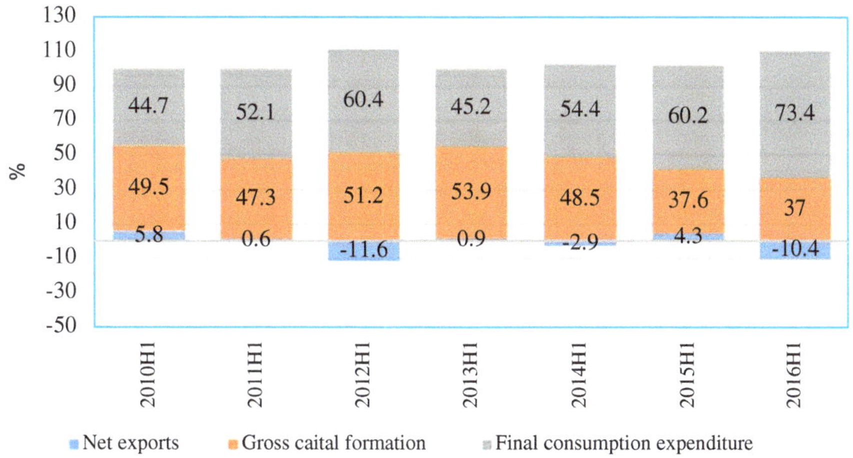

Fig. 1.2 Consumption's contribution to GDP growth increased. *Source* CQMM team calculations on CEIC data

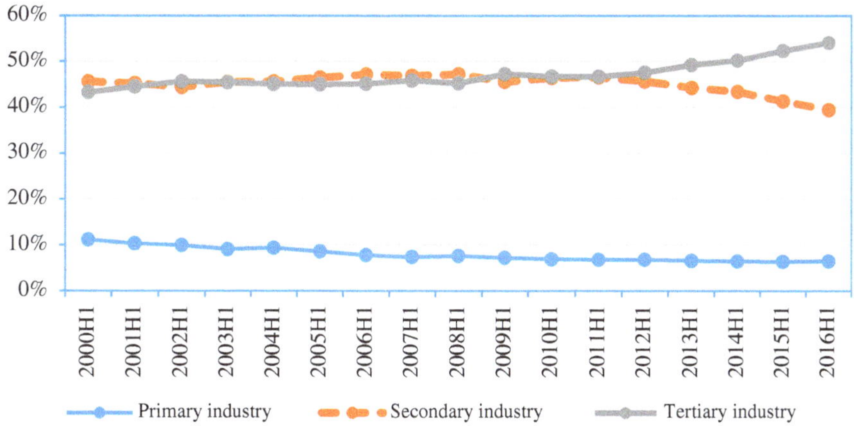

Fig. 1.3 The services industry kept growing YoY. *Source* CQMM team calculations on CEIC data

down by 0.05 and 0.01 over a year-ago period respectively, suggesting some more bitter job competition (Fig. 1.5).

Fourthly, the achievement of supply-side structural reform is being reflected in uptick of corporate returns. In the first half of 2016, among those industries with rampant overcapacity, coal production dropped by 9.0% YoY, crude steel production declined by 2.5%, electrolytic aluminum production fell by 1.8%, plate

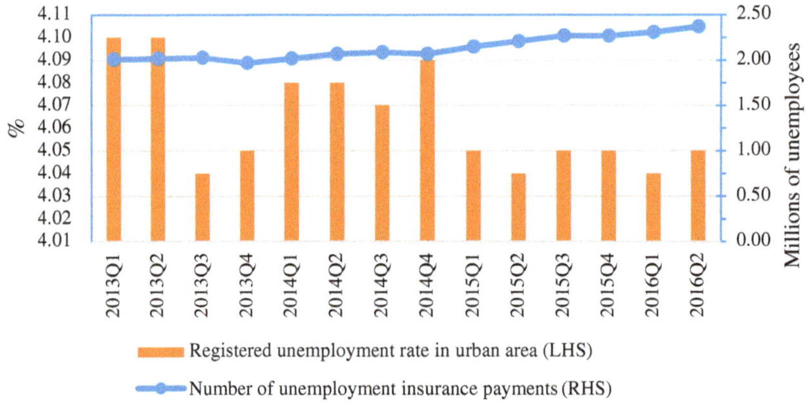

Fig. 1.4 Unemployment rate in urban areas remained stable. *Source* CQMM team calculations on Wind Info data

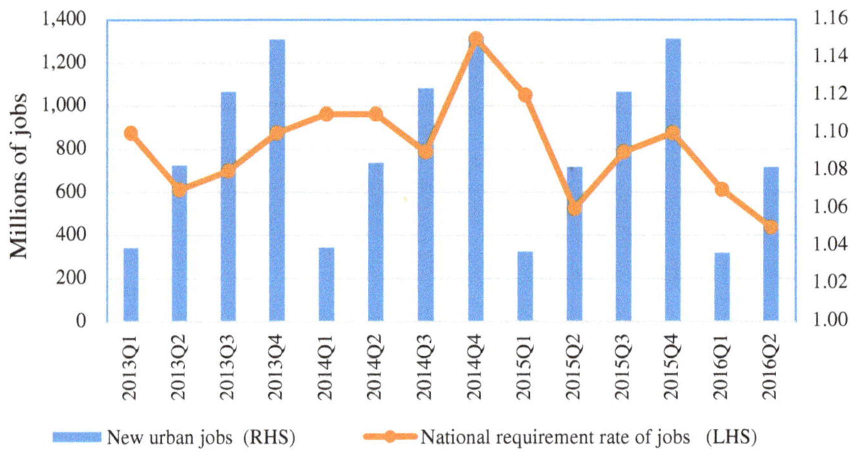

Fig. 1.5 Labor market robustness still in evident. *Source* CQMM team calculations on Wind Info data

glass production was down by 3.6%, while only cement production expanded by 3.0% (see Fig. 1.6). By contrast, production of overall industrial sectors rose by an impressive 6.1%. These figures suggest that measures to cut excess capacity in manufacturing sector has come into force.

In the meantime, supported by measures to reduce businesses cost burden, industrial production picked up slightly, and the financial performance of enterprises improved. In the first half of 2016, of the industrial enterprises above designated size, real industrial value added in real term expanded by 6.0% YoY, 0.2

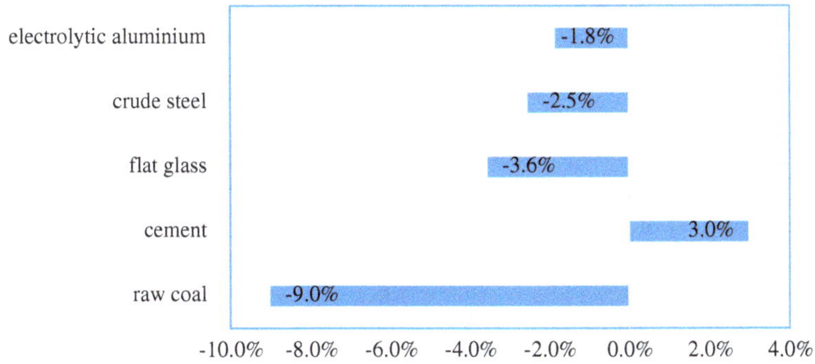

Fig. 1.6 Measures to curb overcapacity came into force YoY. *Source* CQMM team calculations on CEIC data

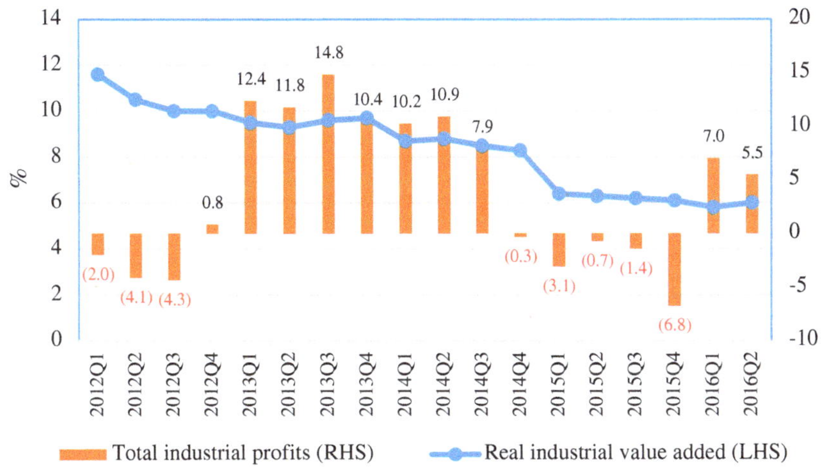

Fig. 1.7 The industry sector gained momentum YoY. *Source* CQMM team calculations on CEIC data

percentage points higher than that in the first quarter. In addition, total profit rose by 5.5%, reversing the continued decline last year (see Fig. 1.7).[2]

Furthermore, manufacturing composition carried on continuous improvement, and growth rates of profit maintained stable. In the first half of 2016, the industrial value added of general-purpose machinery manufacturing sectors increased by 1 percentage points over the same period last year, the growth rate of export delivery value rose by 6.24 percentage points, the growth rate of revenue from principal

[2]The growth rate of profit of industrial enterprises above designated size was down by 6.18% in 2015.

business climbed by 1.05 percentage points, and the growth rate of profit expanded by 1.12 percentage points. The growth rate of industrial value added of special-purpose machinery manufacturing sectors increased by 2.2 percentage points over the same period last year, the growth rate of export delivery value increased by 10 percentage points, the growth rate of revenue from principal business went up by 2.26 percentage points, and the growth rate of profit picked by 10.22 percentage points. The industrial value added of electrical machinery and equipment manufacturing sectors increased by 1.7 percentage points over the same period last year, the growth rate of export delivery value rose by 7.39 percentage points, the growth rate of revenue from principal business climbed by 2.86 percentage points, and the growth rate of profit expanded by 11.98 percentage points.

The transformation and upgrading of industrial structure accelerated, and the newly-emerging strategic industries grew rapidly. In the first half of 2016, the value added for newly-emerging strategic industries, such as energy saving and environmental protection, new generation information technology, bioindustry, high-end equipment manufacturing, new energy, new materials, and new energy vehicles, increased by 11% YoY, 5 percentage points higher than that for overall industrial sectors.

1.2 Total Investment Growth Edged Down While Private Investment Growth Dropped Dramatically

In the first half of 2016, the FAI (excluding rural households) increased by 9.0%, a decline of 2.5 percentage points over the same period last year. Of which, the FAI in the primary industry fell by 6.7 percentage points, the FAI in the secondary industry declined by 4.9 percentage points, and the FAI in the tertiary industry dropped by 0.7 percentage points. Of the FAI in the secondary industry, for mining markedly fell by 12 percentage points over the same period last year, for manufacturing contracted by 6.4 percentage points. Of the FAI in the tertiary industry, for transport, storage and post was down by 8.9 percentage points, for financial sector decreased by 9.2 percentage points, while for real estate picked up by 1.5 percentage points.

In terms of investment composition, the FAI in manufacturing grew by 3.3% YoY, a decrease of 6.4 percentage points over a year earlier. The FAI in real estate development increased by 7.2%, 1.5 percentage points higher than that in the same period last year. The FAI in infrastructure picked up by 20.9%, an increase of 1.1 percentage points over a year ago.

The rapid growth of infrastructure investment and the steady growth of real estate buffered the decelerated growth of overall investment. Of the FAI in the first half of 2016, the share of manufacturing investment is 31.8%, down by 6.4 percentage points over a year earlier, the share of property investment is 23.8%, up by 1.4 percentage points, and the share of infrastructure investment is 24.7%, up by 1.1 percentage points (see Fig. 1.8).

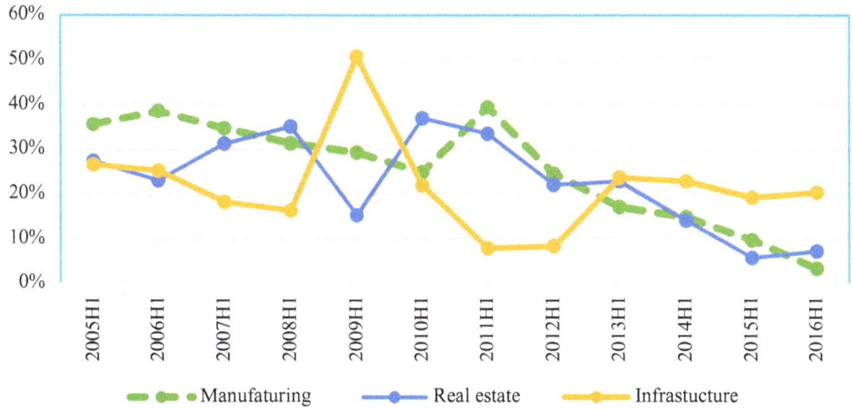

Fig. 1.8 Manufacturing investment slowed down YoY. *Source* CQMM team calculations on CEIC data

The first half of 2016 saw the dramatic drop in private investment growth, which was one of significant characteristics of China's investment growth. In 2015, the private FAI went up by 10.0% YoY, almost matching the 10.1% growth rate of the total FAI. Nevertheless, the gap between the private investment growth and the total investment growth has been widened since early 2016. In the first half of 2016, the private investment growth decelerated by 2.8%, 6.2 percentage points lower than that of the total FAI over the same period last year (see Fig. 1.9).[3]

In addition, the continued slowdown of China's investment growth is not only due to the decelerating private investment growth, but own to a mix of other various factors as follows.

First, in the first half of 2015 and 2016, the total FAI in China reached 23.71 trillion yuan and 25.8 trillion yuan respectively. The huge base reigned the rapid growth of new investment.

Second, mining, in which the coal industry plays an important role, is one of main sectors that the government determined to cut overcapacity. In the first half of 2016, the investment in mining fell by 19.7% YoY, a decrease of 12 percentage points over the same period last year.

Thirdly, China's outward foreign direct investment (OFDI) grew rapidly. In the first half of 2016, the non-financial OFDI reached 88.86 billion dollars, exceeding the FDI for the first time by 19.44 billion dollars on a similar comparison. The non-financial OFDI increased by 58.7% YoY, a significant increase of 29.5 percentage points over a year earlier. Of this, the non-financial OFDI of the first and second quarter picked up by 55.4 and 61.4% respectively, far exceeding the average growth rate of the last five years. Nonetheless, growth of OFDI all dropped

[3]The dramatic drop in private investment growth has raised much concerns. Chapter 3 is to analyses its causes and simulate its macroeconomic effects. Chapter 4 makes corresponding policy suggestions.

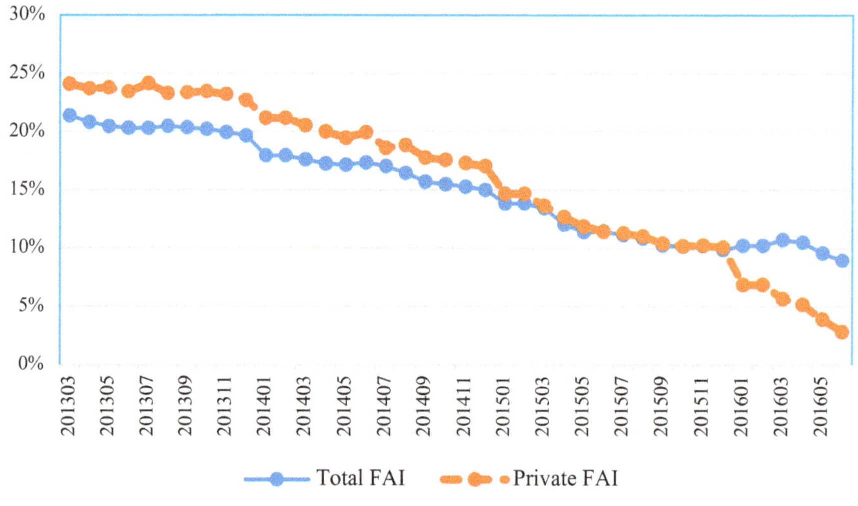

Fig. 1.9 Private investment growth dropped dramatically YoY. *Source* CQMM team calculations on CEIC data

dramatically in the second half of the years since 2012, except 2014 (see Fig. 1.10). Furthermore, although the private outward investment growth accelerated in the first half of 2016, the large and medium state-owned enterprises were still the main forces of China's OFDI, while not private enterprises.[4] So it is hard to tell that there is necessary connection between the rapid growth of OFDI and the sharp drop in private investment growth.

Fourthly, in terms of region, the slowdown of total investment growth was mostly affected by the sharp fall in investment growth in the northeast region.[5] In the first half of 2016, the northeast region, which once was China's most important

[4]According to the *Statistical Communiqué of the People's Republic of China on the 2014 National Outward Foreign Direct Investment* released by the Department of Outward Investment and Economic Cooperation, the OFDI by China central enterprises almost accounted for 48.9% of the total non-financial OFDI. Taking into account the OFDI by local SOEs, the OFDI by SOEs would be the main body of total OFDI. Take Shanghai, in which private investment is relatively concentrated on. The OFDI by SOEs in 2014 reached 5.28 billion dollars, accounting for 42.93% of total investment. In addition, in terms of volume of projects, for SOEs are commonly greater than those for private enterprises. Source: Shanghai Municipality Commission, Annual Report on Shanghai OFDI Cooperation and Development 2015.

[5]The eastern region covers ten provinces or municipalities: Beijing, Tianjin, Hebei, Shanghai, Jiangsu, Zhejiang, Fujian, Shandong, and Hainan. The central region covers six provinces: Shanxi, Anhui, Jiangxi, Henan, Hubei, and Hunan. The western region covers twelve provinces, municipalities, or autonomous region: Inner Mongolia, Guangxi, Chongqing, Sichuan, Guizhou, Yunnan, Tibet, Shaanxi, Gansu, Qinghai, Ningxia, and Xinjiang. The northeastern region covers three provinces: Liaoning, Jilin, and Heilongjiang. In December, 2015, the FAI in the three provinces in the northeastern region was first listed independently by the National Bureau of Statistics (NBS).

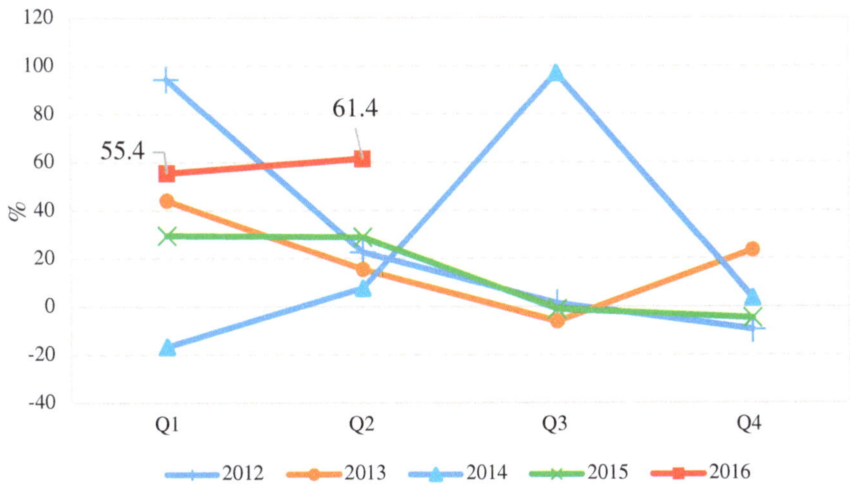

Fig. 1.10 Growth rates of non-financial OFDI QoQ. *Source* CQMM team calculations on CEIC data

manufacturing base, has been significantly affected by measures to eliminate backward production capacity. The FAI growth in northeast region declined by 32% YoY, a decrease of 20.8 percentage points over a year earlier. In contrast, the investment growth in other regions maintained relatively stable. Of the FAI growth, the eastern region climbed by 11% YoY, the central region rose by 12.8%, and the western region went up by 13.5% (see Fig. 1.11). After excluding the northeast region, in the first half of 2016, China would see a 12.3% growth rate of investment, only dropped by 0.4 percentage points over the same period last year.[6]

Nonetheless, while China's total investment growth edged down, its structure was improved. In terms of industrial sector, the increasing share of investment in high-tech industry will help the industrial sector move forward to medium-end and high-end industries. In the first half of 2016, high-tech industry investment grew by 13.1% YoY, 4.1 percentage points higher than the total FAI growth rates. The ratio of high-tech industry investment to total FAI is 6%, 0.2 percentage points higher than that in the same period last year. Of investment in services sectors, investment in high-tech services sectors accelerated. In the first half of 2016, high-tech services investment expanded by 16.4% YoY, 4.7 percentage points higher than that in services investment. In addition, the investment in some sectors related to people's livelihood also grew rapidly. For examples, the investment in management of water conservancy, environment and public facilities increased by 26.7% YoY, and the investment in science, education, culture, and health rose 18.1%, 13.4 and 5 percentage points higher than that in total services investment respectively.

[6]CQMM team calculations on CEIC data.

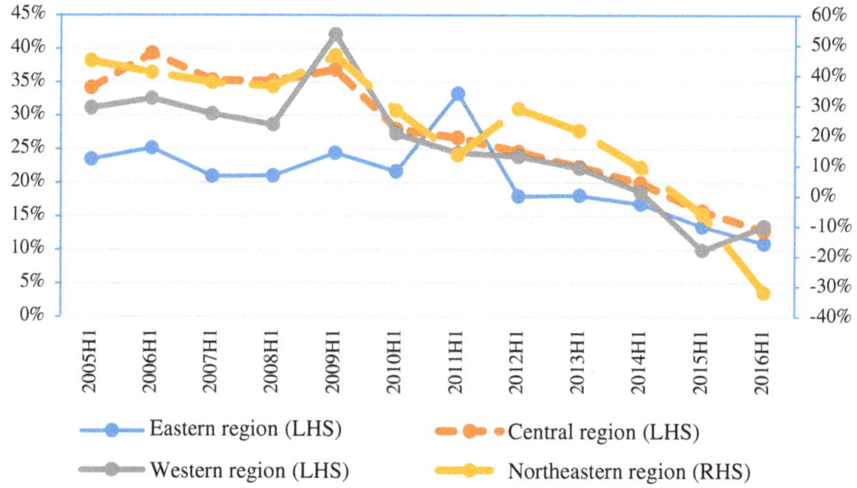

Fig. 1.11 The FAI in the northeastern region fell sharply YoY. *Source* CQMM team calculations on CEIC data

It is noteworthy that the accelerating infrastructure investment was mostly financed by public funds. Besides, given that the real estate is undergoing destocking in many cities, it might be a temporary choice to support the total investment growth by property investment. Taking into account China's high governmental and corporate leverage, it would be difficult to maintain the total investment by boosting infrastructure and property investment. The growth of investment in the second half of 2016 is expected to decelerate.

1.3 Consumption Growth Remained Steady Despite Household Income Growth Decelerated

Coinciding with the economy's downward trend, the household income subdued. In the first half of 2016, China's per capita real disposable income of households increased by 6.5% YoY, 1.1 percentage points lower than that in the same period last year. Quarterly, it rose 6.5% both in the first and second quarter, 0.2 percentage points lower than the GDP growth rate on a similar comparison, which occurred for the first time in recent years (see Fig. 1.12).

In the first half of 2016, sales of consumer goods at domestic market increased steadily. Total retail sales of consumer goods picked up by 10.3% YoY, matching its growth rate in the first half of 2015. Given weak foreign trade and subdued investment growth, the steadily rapid growth of household consumption increased the contribution of consumption to GDP growth. In the first half of 2016, the contribution of final consumption expenditure accounts for 73.4% of GDP growth,

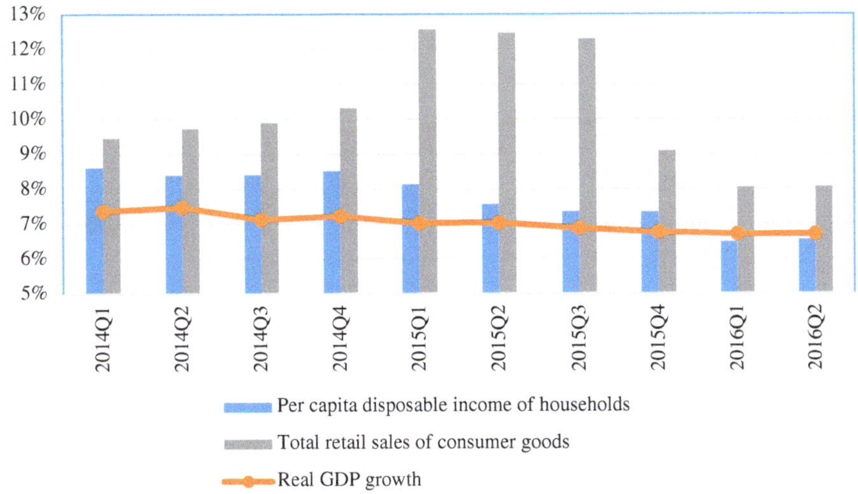

Fig. 1.12 Consumption growth stayed robust YoY. *Source* CQMM team calculations on CEIC data

an increase of 13.2 percentage points over the same period a year ago and 13.5 percentage points over 2015 respectively.

While sales of consumer goods expanded, new commercial forms grew rapidly. In the first half of 2016, the online retail sales[7] of physical goods increased by 26.6%, accounting for 11.6% of the total retail sales of consumer goods, up by 0.8 percentage points than that in 2015. Furthermore, sales of quality consumer goods maintained rapid growth, suggesting that the consumption structure be upgraded distinctively, In the first half of 2016, of retail sales by enterprises above designated size, for sports and recreation articles went up by 16.9% YoY, for communication equipment grew by 14.9%, for camera increased by 22%, all above the growth rate of total retail sales of consumer goods, suggesting that the demand for consumer goods is being upgraded.

Consumption in rural areas grew faster than that in urban areas. In the first quarter and the second quarter, the real retail sales of consumer goods in rural area were up by 8.8 and 8.6%, 0.9 and 0.7 percentage points higher than those in urban areas respectively, maintaining the state of growing faster than that in urban areas since 2013. The narrowing gap between the urban-rural consumption growth is coinciding with figures for the urban-rural income gap. In the first and second quarter, the per capita real disposable income of rural residents went up by 7.0 and

[7]Online Retail Sales: refers to the sales of goods and services got through public online trading platform (including self-built websites and third-party platform). Goods and services include physical goods and non-physical goods (such as virtual product, services). The total retail sales of consumer goods include online retail sales of physical goods, excludes online retail sales of non-physical goods.

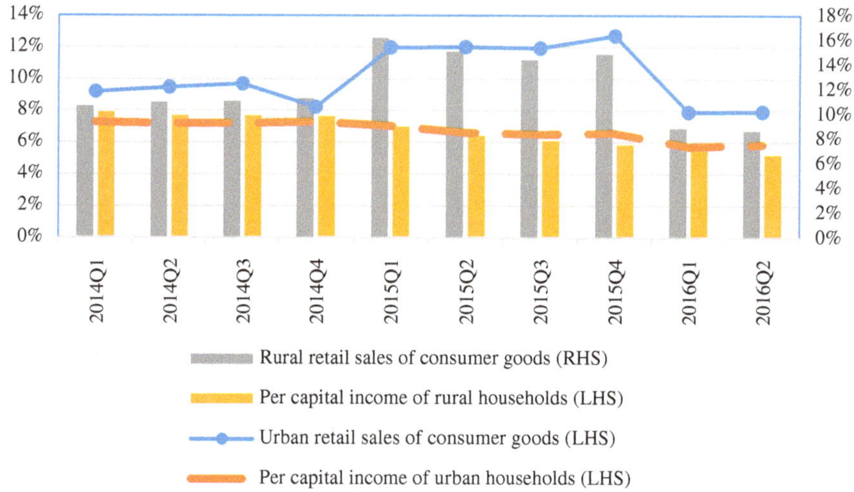

Fig. 1.13 Consumption in rural areas grew faster than than in urban areas YoY. *Source* CQMM team calculations on CEIC data

6.7% respectively. By contrast, the per capita real disposable income of urban households picked up by 5.7 and 5.8% respectively (see Fig. 1.13). Helped by the internet platform, the consumption market in rural areas has been extended, and the consumption environment has been improved. Compared with urban areas, the market structure of consumer goods in rural areas has larger development room.

1.4 Foreign Trade Growth Remained Sluggish

Global trade remains very subdued in the first half of 2016. According to the update forecast released by the International Monetary Funds (IMF) on July 19, 2016, the growth rate of global trade in goods and services is expected to be 2.7%, only slightly up by 0.1 percentage points over last year. Owing to the weak external demand and outward transfer of industries, China's export remained sluggish. In the first half of 2016, the total value of exports in dollar terms dropped by 7.7% YoY, down by 8.6 percentage points over the same period last year (see Fig. 1.14). By country and region, the decline of exports is closely related to that of exports to the US and the ASEAN. In the first half of 2016, the value of exports to the US and the ASEAN dropped by 9.9 and 8.4% respectively, while the value of exports to these two regions accounts for 30.1% of total value. In terms of type of trade, the processing trade exports fell by 9.9% YoY, while the general trade exports decreased by 7.7%.

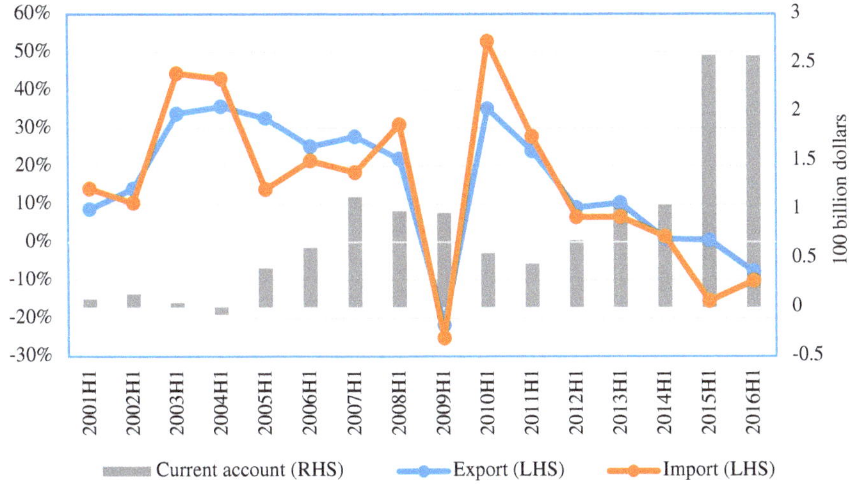

Fig. 1.14 Foreign trade growth remained weak YoY. *Source* CQMM team calculations on CEIC data

In the near term, the external demand will remain weak. Such great events as Brexit, the South China Sea event, and the pickup of international trade protectionism, are expected to put pressures on exports. Though the continued RMB depreciation is expected to support exports, generally speaking, it is hard to be optimistic about China's export prospects.

Owing to economic slowdown and no significant improvement in domestic demand, imports continued to hover low. In the first half of 2016, the total value of imports in dollar term dropped by 10.2% YoY, the rate of decline slowed by 5.4 percentage points over the same period last year (see Fig. 1.14). As bulk commodities account for a large proportion of China's imported commodities, with the decline in prices for imported bulk commodities slowed, the fall in total value of imports eased correspondingly. In the first half of 2016, of the average import prices, the rate of decline in iron ore slowed by 23.3 percentage points over 2015, in crude oil slowed by 13.4 percentage points, in coal slowed by 1.7 percentage points, and in copper slowed by 1.7 percentage points. The increase in both volumes and prices of imported bulk commodities eased falls in the total value of imports.

In terms of merchandise, mechanical and electrical products and traditional labor-intensive products are still the main categories of exports, though the growth rates of them decreased simultaneously. In the first half of 2016, the value of exports in dollar term for mechanical and electrical products fell by 8.0% YoY, accounting for 57.2% of the total value of exports. Of this total, for integrated circuit increased by 2.9%, for solar batteries export expanded by 1.9%. The value of exports for traditional labor-intensive products dropped by 5.1%, accounting for 21% of the total value of export. Of this total, for toys grew by 8.9%, while for textile, wearing apparel, and plastics only fell slightly, suggesting that some traditional products still maintained their competitiveness.

1.5 The CPI Sustained Stable While the Decline in PPI Slowed

In the first half of 2016, the consumer price index (CPI) rose by 2.1% YoY, meaning mild consumer price inflation. Even though the rapid growth of bank credit and money supply heightened the pressure on consumer price inflation, after the second quarter of 2016, the vegetable prices dropped much more than expected, and the growth of pork prices slowed down, the inflation pressure shown up in the first quarter started to ease. No-food price index maintained stable, its growth rates has steadily stayed in the range of 0.9–1.2% in the past sixteen months. In addition, the core CPI performed stable too, its growth rates slightly fluctuate between 1.3 and 1.6% in the last 17 months (see Fig. 1.15).

Since early 2016, due to the property boom in upper-tier cities and the accelerating implementation of programmed infrastructure projects, prices of bulk commodities had a sharp rebound. Falls in the producer price index (PPI) have been eased from down by 5.9% in August, 2015, to down by 2.6% in June, 2016. Over the same period, the rate of decline in the PPI for means of production has slowed from down by 7.7 to 3.5%, and that in the PPI for consumer goods has slowed from down by 0.3–0.1% (see Fig. 1.16).

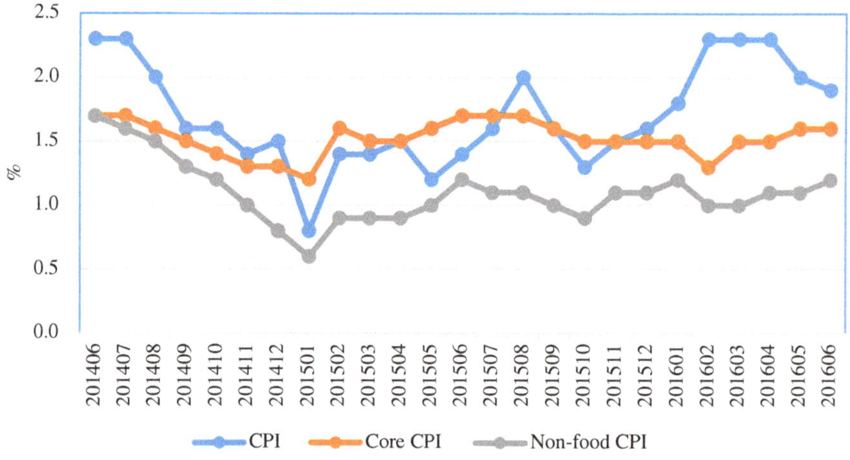

Fig. 1.15 Inflation pressure subdued YoY. *Source* CQMM team calculations on CEIC data

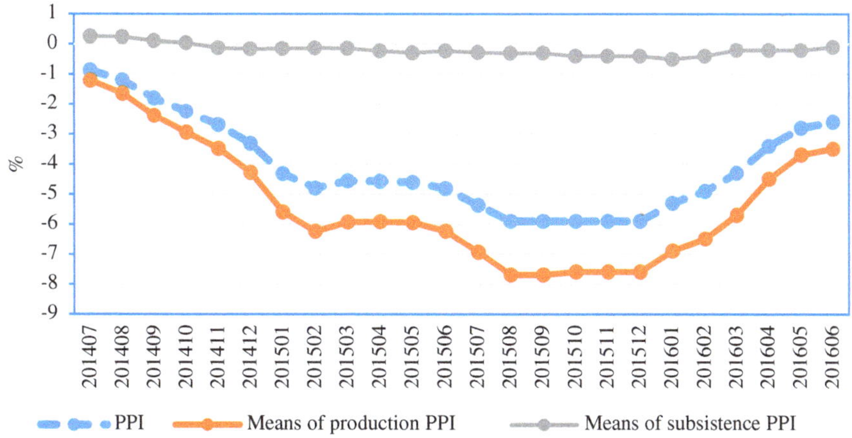

Fig. 1.16 Decline in PPI eased YoY. *Source* CQMM team calculations on CEIC data

1.6 Bank Credit Rose Rapidly While the Gap Between M1 and M2 Growth Widened

In the first half of 2016, the new loan amounted to 7.53 trillion yuan, about 1 trillion yuan more than that in the same period last year. Of this total, growth of loans of non-financial enterprises and loans of government department and organizations maintained steady compared to a year earlier. The additional 1 trillion yuan loans were all from household sector. Of new loans from household, the medium and long-term loans increased by 2.62 trillion yuan, 1.28 trillion yuan higher, or an increase of 95.52%, over the same period last year. As the medium and long-term household loans mainly consists of mortgage, the likely explanation is that, in the first half of 2016, the property boom in upper-tier cities brought a surge in bank credit, and then the surge in bank credit spurred the housing market in turn, resulting in the property boom.

By the end of June, 2016, the narrow money (M1) went up by 24.6% YoY, and the broad money (M2) picked up by 11.8%, meaning that the growth rate of M1 is 12.8 percentage points higher than that of M2. Actually, the growth of M1 started to exceed that of M2 in October, 2015. Since then, the scissors difference between them has been widened continuously. The difference increased to 12.8 percentage points at the end of June, 2016, from 0.5 percentage points at the end of October, 2015 (see Fig. 1.17).

The M2 growth slowed down for the following reasons:

- Balance of M2 has been great.
- The sharp drop in the bank acceptance bill brought about a significant fall in corporate margin deposits.

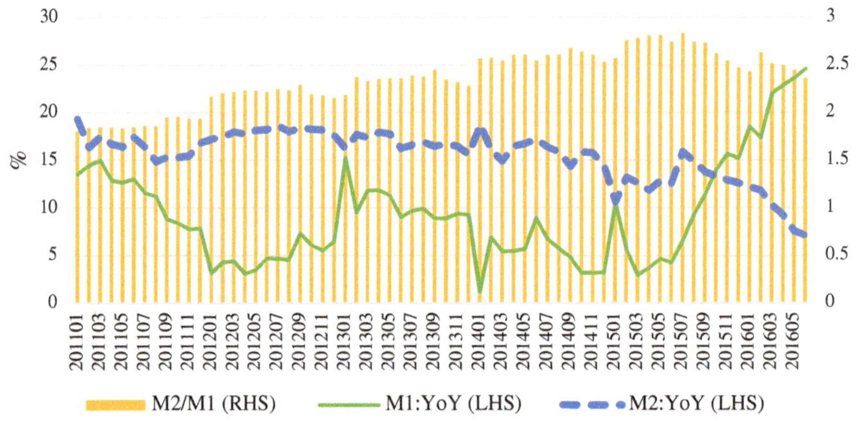

Fig. 1.17 The scissors difference between M1 and M2 growth widened. *Source* CQMM team calculations on CEIC data

- Composition for foreign exchanges purchase declined continuously, making derived deposits fall.
- Large amount of local government bonds issued drained much bank fund and crowded out bank loans to certain degree, weakening the ability of banking system to create money.

As to the increasingly rapid growth of M1, one cause is that the corporate demand deposits expanded significantly. To be specific, first, the interest rate differential between time deposits and demand deposits narrowed, the opportunity cost of holding demand deposit declined. Second, many companies tend to hold money, waiting for investment opportunities. And thirdly, hot property sales led the household deposits and the housing mortgage loans to real estate enterprises demand deposits.

The other cause is that, due to the large number of local government replacement bonds issued in the first half of 2016, some funds from local government replacement bonds and newly issued bonds retained temporarily were put in the bank accounts of government departments and organizations (most of them are local government financing vehicles accounts), which increased significantly the demand deposits by government departments and organizations.

According to the plan by China's central government, 11.4 trillion RMB yuan worth of local government bonds is to be replaced in 2016 and 2017, suggesting that the annual average is 5.7 trillion yuan. In the first half of 2016, the replacement bonds publicly issued and directional issue amounted to 2.65 trillion yuan in total, suggesting that the send half of 2016 will see 3.05 trillion yuan of replacement bonds newly issued. Thus, the gap between M1 and M2 growth rate is expected to be widened.

The above analysis shows that, the sharp increase of bank credit and the divergence between M1 and M2 in the first half of 2016, closely related to the property boom. And the property investment growth, spurred by the property boom, has played an important role in supporting China's economic growth. However, on a fundamental basis, assets prices cannot be divorced from the real economy, otherwise financial risks would be accumulated constantly. In addition, if assets prices go up rapidly, then prices of other materials, or even the price indices, would be stimulated, which would put the implementation of monetary policy in a dilemma.

As for as real estate, the goals of its policy in the second half of 2016 should constrain too rapid growth in upper-tier cities on one side, and to destock the overstocking houses in lower-tier cities on the other side. That implies that there is a tradeoff between controlled the overhung property prices and destocking. Extending this idea to the aggregate economy, the monetary policy in the second half of 2016 should also make tradeoff between stabilizing decelerating economic growth and promote structural transformation, while addressing the financial stability risks.

1.7 Fiscal Revenues Saw Fast Growth and Fiscal Expenditures Expanded Dramatically

In the first half of 2016, the property boom in upper-tier cities brought about the pickup of fiscal revenues. The national general public budget revenues amounted to 8.55 trillion yuan, up by 7.1% YoY (6.8% in real term). Of this total, the central general public budget revenues reached 3.72 trillion yuan, up by 3.3%, and the local general public budget revenues reached 4.84 trillion yuan, up by 10.1%.

Of the national general public budget revenues, the total tax revenues increased by 8.6% (8.0% in real term) YoY, exceeding the GDP growth rate of 7.2% (6.7% in real term), reversing the situation that tax growth lagged GDP growth in 2015 (see Fig. 1.18). The main reason is that the surge of property prices in the upper-tier cities led to the increase of those taxes directly related to real estate. For instance, contract tax went up by 14.8% YoY, the land VAT picked up by 13.1%, and housing property tax rose 8.5%. The property boom also spurred the expansion of those taxes indirectly connected to real estate, say, corporate income tax, VAT, business tax, personal income tax, and so on. For instance, corporate income tax from real estate increased by 17.3%, and income tax from transfer of property grew by 23.9%.

Property boom in upper-tier cities spurred the land market, driving the land concession fee grow rapidly. In the first half of 2016, the local government land concession fee reached 1.43 trillion yuan, up by 9.7% YoY, a sharp increase of 48.0 percentage points over the same period last year. As the land concession fee accounts for over 75% of local government funds revenues, the latter, which works as the second largest Source of local government revenues, picked up by 5.7%, a significant increase of 38.9 percentage points over the same period last year (see Fig. 1.19).

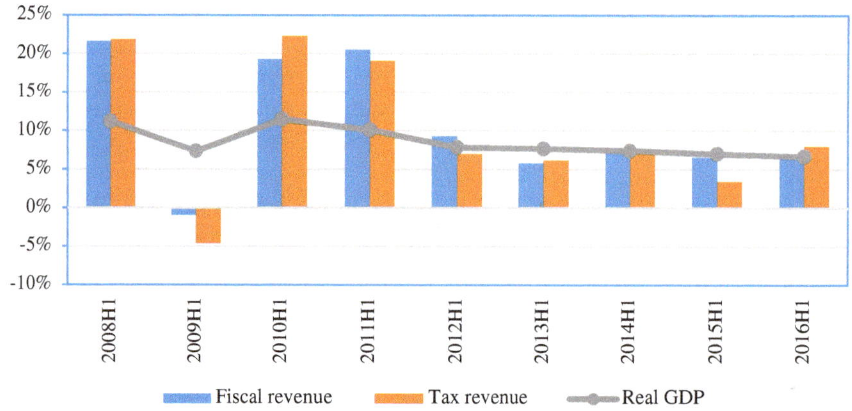

Fig. 1.18 Fiscal revenues growth accelerated YoY. *Source* CQMM team calculations on CEIC data

China expanded the pilot program of replacing business tax with value-added tax (VAT) on May 1, 2016. Such a move was implemented due to the following three reasons:

- To avoid repeat tax levy to promote specialized division of labor.
- To link together the broken tax chain between the industrial sector and services while the two sectors have become more closely interwined.
- To reduce the business cost by relieving the tax burden, where the move is considered as part of the supply-side structural reform.

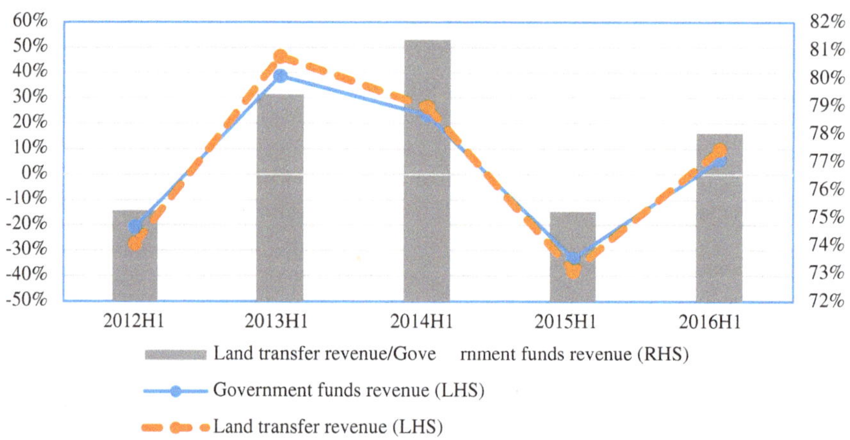

Fig. 1.19 Fast-growing land concess fee increased goverment funds revenues YoY. *Source* CQMM team calculations on CEIC data

It will take time to evaluate the real effects of such a tax reform. It's now the case that, in the first half of 2016, the domestic VAT increased by 8.7%. In terms of month, it grew by 20.9% in June, an increase of 15.1 percentage points over the first five months of 2016. In the meantime, as original business taxpayers turned to pay VAT, business tax dropped by 86% in June, while the total business tax went up by 15.6% in the first half of 2016.

The change in tax structure reflects that China's industry structure is being upgraded. In the first half of 2016, tax from the services industry rose 10.9% YoY, accounting for 58.2% of total tax revenues, 2.2 percentage points higher than that in the same period last year. In addition, tax from newly-emerging services sectors grew rapidly. Of this, tax from software and information technology services rose 39% YoY, where tax from leasing and business services sectors increased by 27.7%, suggesting that it is an important driver to boost tax growth in the services industry. Furthermore, tax from high-end manufacturing saw fast growth as well, suggesting the effects of innovation improved. Of this, tax from space equipment manufacturing climbed 11.1%, tax from pharmaceutical manufacturing and automobile manufacturing grew by 12.2 and 7.2% respectively.

In terms of region, in the first half of 2016, the growth rates of tax from the eastern region, the central region and the western region, are 12.2, 4.9, and 4.4% respectively. As modern services industry and high-end manufacturing are mainly located in the eastern regions, from which more tax revenues can be created by these fast-growing industries, making the growth rate of tax from the eastern region is persistently faster than those from the central and western regions.

To meet demands for ensuring people's livelihood and stabilizing economic growth, fiscal expenditure maintained fast growth in the first half of 2016, up by 15.4% over the same period last year, 8 percentage points higher than the growth rate of fiscal revenues (see Fig. 1.20). The central government general public

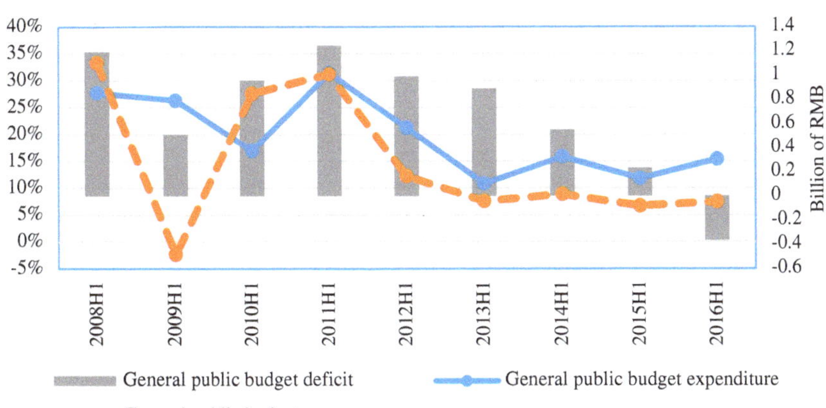

Fig. 1.20 Fiscal expenditure growth overtook fiscal revenues growth YoY. *Source* CQMM team calculations on CEIC data

budget expenditure rose 7.2% YoY, and the local government central general public budget expenditure climbed 16.6. The main target of general public budget expenditure was on satisfying people's livelihood. For instance, expenditures on urban and rural communities went up by 34.5%, expenditures on housing security picked up by 27.5%, expenditures on public health and family planning expanded by 23.7%, expenditures on education increased by 16.7%, expenditures for social security and employment rose 15%, and interest payments on debt climbed 38.1%.

In the first half of 2016, fiscal deficit amounted to 36.51 billion yuan. China's budgetary deficit in 2016 reaches 2.18 trillion, meaning that the room for fiscal deficit is about 1.8 trillion yuan in the second half of 2016. As downward pressure on the economy persists, fiscal revenues is expected to slow down, while fiscal expenditure is expected to expand to support economic growth, suggesting that fiscal deficit in the second half of 2016 increase much more than that in the first half of 2016.

In summary, the first half of 2016 saw the continued slowdown of China's economic growth. Given the relatively steady growth of consumption and persistently subdued foreign trade, the deceleration of total investment growth was the key factor of economic slowdown. Due to measures to curb excess capacity, investment in mining industry dropped sharply, and manufacturing investment growth edged down. High corporate leverage and the decline of profit growth weakened investment willingness among businesses. And the sharp drop of private investment growth reflects the lack of inner motive of endogenous investment growth. For these reasons, the downward trend in total investment growth would not be offset by either the property investment growth supported by credit expansion or the accelerating infrastructure investment growth led by the government, or both. In the second half of 2016, total investment growth is expected to slow down further, and marginal effects of investment on economic growth continue fading.

Since the global financial crises, due to the dramatic changes in the domestic and international economic environment, the previous investment-driven and export-oriented growth pattern, featured by both export and investment driven, has become unsustainable. Given sluggish external demand and increasing costs of production factors, it is urgent for China to change its current growth pattern. China's macroeconomic policy has to make a difficult tradeoff between near-term demand management measures and long-term supply-side structural transformation, while in the meantime addressing financial stability risks.

Nevertheless, during China's transition from a high-middle income country to a high-income country, the domestic demand structure is being updated, and the contribution of consumption to economic growth is rising. All these have brought about not only continuous expansion of the services industry, but constant adjustment of industrial structure to meet the transformation of demand structure. And the impact of decelerating economic growth on labor markets has been so far relatively small due to the continuous expansion of the services industry. Furthermore, measures to cut backward production capacity have come into force.

Supported by various policies to reduce business cost burden, industrial production picked up slightly, and financial performance of enterprises began to improve. Manufacturing structure carries on continuous improvement, and its growth rate of profit tends to be stable. Transformation and upgrading of the industrial structure are accelerating, and the newly-emerging strategic industries grow rapidly.

In the long run, the positive effects of structural transformation would become the fundamental forces to stabilize China's economic growth.

Chapter 2
Quarterly Forecast for 2016–17

2.1 Assumptions on Exogenous Variables

2.1.1 Growth Rates of the United States and the Euro Area

The outcome of the UK vote to exit from the European Union in June 23, 2016, has reinforced uncertainty about the global outlook for 2016-17 and increased expectations of more easing monetary policy in advanced economies. According the *World Economic Outlook Update (WEO Update)* released by the International Monetary Fund (IMF) on July 19, 2017, the US economic growth is forecast at 2.2% in 2016 and 2.5% in 2017. However, the real GDP growth rate in the second quarter released recently is only 1.1%, less than half of the market expectation. Taking this into account, even though the US economy growth is being on a steadily upward trend, forecasts for 2016 and 2017 are both marked down by 0.2 percentage points relative to the July 2016 *WEO Update* by the IMF, to 2 and 2.3%, respectively.

In addition, according to the *WOE Update*, we assume that the euro area GDP growth are expected to go up by 1.6% in 2016 and 1.4% in 2017. Quarterly, the US and euro area growth rates are shown in Fig. 2.1.

2.1.2 The Exchange Rates

Since 2015, China's benchmark lending rates have been cut five times by the central bank, fiscal policy has turned expansionary, infrastructure spending has gone up, and credit growth has accelerated. Now that newly issued money has

Center for Macroeconomic Research of Xiamen University,
China's Macroeconomic Outlook, Current Chinese Economic
Report Series, DOI 10.1007/978-981-10-3280-6_2

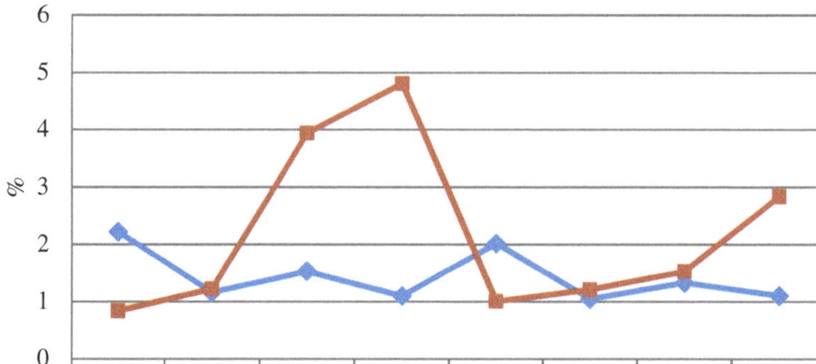

	2016Q1	2016Q2	2016Q3	2016Q4	2017Q1	2017Q2	2017Q3	2017Q4
EA_GDP_C	2.2	1.2	1.5	1.1	2.0	1.0	1.3	1.1
USA_GDP_C	0.8	1.2	3.9	4.8	1.0	1.2	1.5	2.8

Fig. 2.1 Assumptions on growth rates in the US and the euro area. Seasonally adjusted QoQ. *Note* EAGDP_C denotes real growth rate in the euro area, and USGDP_C denotes real GDP growth rate in the US. *Source* CQMM team assumptions

increased distinctively, RMB has to bear depreciation pressures. When RMB depreciation triggered notable capital outflows after August, 2015, the intensification of China's capital control subsequently stabilized the RMB. However, though the capital outflows have been slowed, the long-term RMB depreciation expectations remain. The RMB exchange rate is expected to be down to 6.75 yuan and 7.1 yuan against the dollar at the end of 2016 and 2017 respectively.

Given its stance of easing monetary policy and the uncertainty enforced by the UK referendum, the European Central Bank is expected to boost the euro area economy via weak euro. In the meantime, the upward trend in the US economic growth helps to form dollar appreciation expectations. In the second half of 2016, the euro would continue depreciating. The euro is expected to be at 1.08 dollars at the end of 2016 and 1.06 dollars at the end of 2017 respectively (see Fig. 2.2).

2.1.3 Growth Rate of the Broad Money Supply (M2)

China's M2 growth were up by 13.4 and 11.8% in the first and second quarter of 2016 respectively. Given various downward pressures on the economy, in order to meet expectations of China's GDP growth, the central bank is expected to expand the money supply by making one cut in interest rates and one cut in reserve

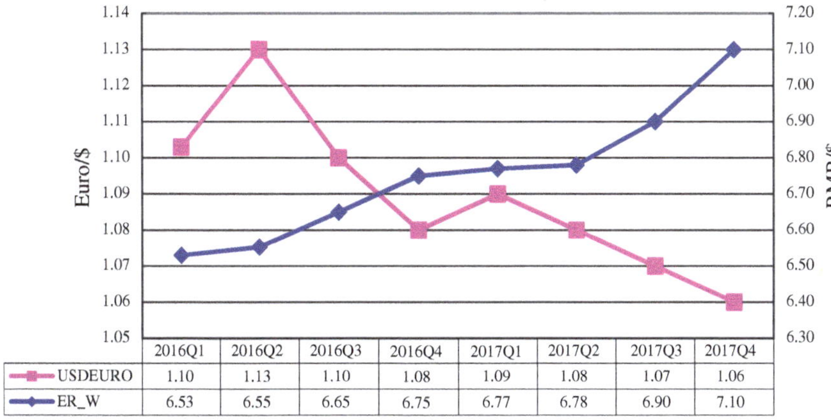

	2016Q1	2016Q2	2016Q3	2016Q4	2017Q1	2017Q2	2017Q3	2017Q4
USDEURO	1.10	1.13	1.10	1.08	1.09	1.08	1.07	1.06
ER_W	6.53	6.55	6.65	6.75	6.77	6.78	6.90	7.10

Fig. 2.2 Assumptions on exchange rates changes. YoY. *Source* CQMM team assumptions

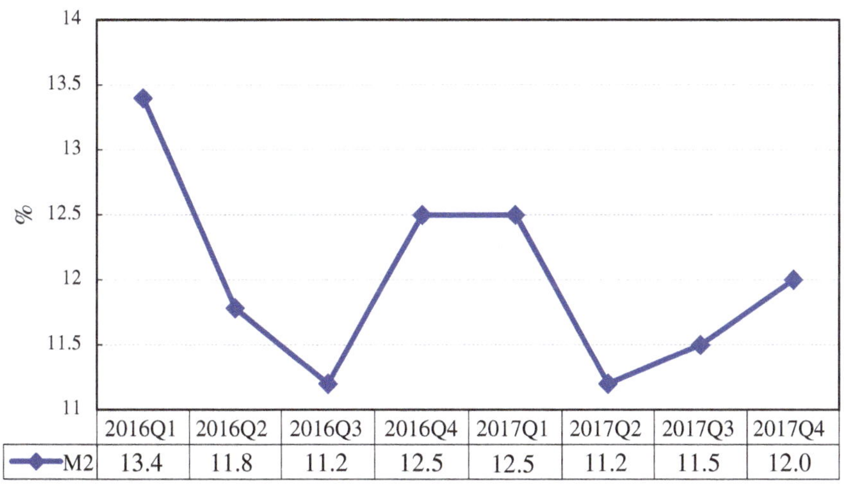

	2016Q1	2016Q2	2016Q3	2016Q4	2017Q1	2017Q2	2017Q3	2017Q4
M2	13.4	11.8	11.2	12.5	12.5	11.2	11.5	12.0

Fig. 2.3 Assumptions on M2 growth rates. YoY. *Source* CQMM team assumptions

requirement ratio. The growth rate of M2 in 2016 is assumed to be at 12.5%. On account of the current large base of M2, which is more than one time over the GDP, and China's central bank is actively trying other ways to increase the social funds, the M2 growth in 2017 is expected to sustain stable at 12% (see Fig. 2.3).

2.2 Quarterly Forecast for China Major Macroeconomic Indicators in 2016–17

2.2.1 GDP Growth Rates

Based on the above assumptions on exogenous variables in the China Quarterly Macroeconometric Model (CQMM), it is forecast that China's GDP growth rate would be 6.63% YoY in 2016, a decrease of 0.27 percentage points over 2015. In 2017, China's economic growth is expected to edge down. The GDP growth is expected to fall to 6.54%, 0.09 percentage points lower than that in 2016.

Quarterly, China's GDP growth is projected to shrink to 6.56 and 6.52% in the third and fourth quarter of 2016 respectively. And thus the whole year of 2016 would see the GDP growth rates showing a downward trend. As to 2017, not only the stimulatory effect of RMB depreciation and slow recovery of US economy on the international side, but the positive effects of industrial structure adjustment on the domestic side, are expected to support bolstering up China's economic growth. The GDP growth in 2017 would be on a high-low trend, up by 6.61% YoY in the first quarter and then slowing down to 6.52% in the fourth quarter (see Fig. 2.4).

2.2.2 Major Prices Indices

According to the CQMM forecasts, the CPI is projected to rise 2.01% YoY, an increase of 0.57 percentage points over 2015, and it would be down to 1.71% in 2017, suggesting that China's inflation is expected to maintain at a steady, moderate pace.

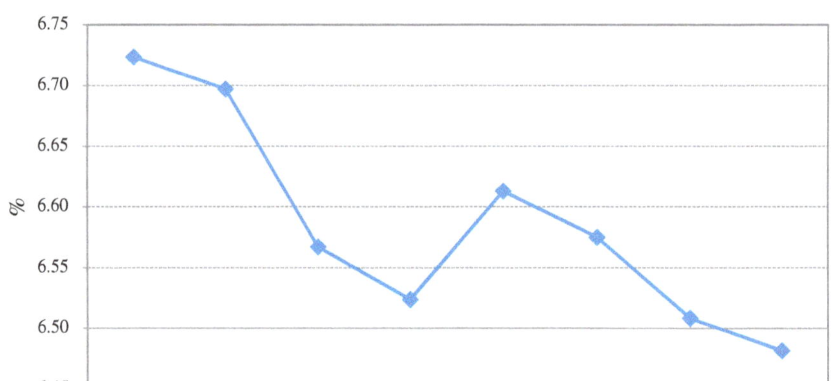

	2016Q1	2016Q2	2016Q3	2016Q4	2017Q1	2017Q2	2017Q3	2017Q4
GDP	6.72	6.70	6.57	6.52	6.61	6.57	6.51	6.48

Fig. 2.4 Projected GDP growth rates, YoY. *Source* CQMM team calculations

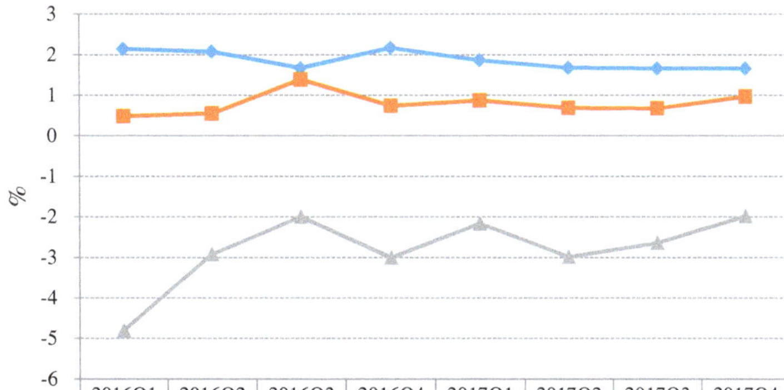

	2016Q1	2016Q2	2016Q3	2016Q4	2017Q1	2017Q2	2017Q3	2017Q4
CPI	2.14	2.07	1.67	2.17	1.86	1.68	1.66	1.65
P_GDP	0.48	0.55	1.38	0.73	0.87	0.68	0.67	0.96
PPI	-4.80	-2.92	-2.00	-3.01	-2.17	-2.99	-2.64	-1.98

Fig. 2.5 Projected growth rates of price indices, YoY. *Note* CPI denotes the consumer prices index, P_GDP denotes the GDP deflator, and PPI denotes the producer price index. *Source* CQMM team calculations

Quarterly, even though the CPI climbed 2.17% in the first quarter of 2016 due to a surge in pork and vegetable prices growth, its growth declined to 2.07%. The CPI growth is projected to continue falling to 1.67% and pick up to 2.17% in the fourth quarter. The decelerating economy growth in 2017 would drag the CPI growth down. The CPI is projected to rise 1.86 and 1.65% in the first and second quarter respectively (see Fig. 2.5).

The producer price index (PPI) is forecast to continue staying in the negative territory, while the decline of rate would slow further. The PPI is projected to fall by 3.19 and 2.45% in 2016 and 2017 respectively. The easing of PPI decline would help improve profits of upstream enterprises in means of production and relieve corporate debt load.

Quarterly, due to the rise of prices in bulk commodities, the decline in PPI in the second quarter of 2016 once slowed, down by 2.92%. Nevertheless, large uncertainty in the bulk commodity prices remains. PPP is projected to decline by 2% in the second quarter, and further drop by 3.01% in the fourth quarter. In 2017, as the measures to cut overcapacity is expected to play a bigger role, the decline in PPI would continue slowing. PPI growth is projected to go down by 1.98% in the fourth quarter of 2017(see Fig. 2.5).

The GDP deflator (P_GDP) is projected to rise by 0.79% in 2016, and the level is to expected to maintain in 2017, suggesting that deflation risks remain low. Quarterly, the GDP deflator slightly picked up in the first half of 2016, and it is expected to maintain modest growth. Due to the pickup of PPI in the third quarter, the GDP deflator is projected to rise by 1.38 and 0.73% in third and fourth quarter respectively. After that, since the decline in the PPI is expected to slow, the GDP deflator is expected to increase, its growth rate is forecast to rise to 0.96% in the fourth quarter of 2017 (see Fig. 2.5).

2.3 Growth Rates of Other Major Macroeconomic Indicators

2.3.1 Growth Rates of Exports, Imports, and Foreign Exchange Reserves

Brexit, together with the much lower-than-expected US GDP growth rate in the second quarter of 2016, heightened uncertainty about the global market. Nevertheless, the effects of RMB depreciation on foreign trade, and the ongoing implementation of "one belt, one road" policy, are expected to offset the downside risks of continued decline in exports. In addition, affected by decelerating domestic economic growth, imports growth would remain sluggish.

According to the CQMM, the total value of exports in dollar term (measured at current price) is forecast to be down by 6.01% in 2016, a drop of 3.79 percentage points over 2015. The total value of imports is projected to be down by 14.12%, matching its 2015 level (see Table 2.1).

Exports growth is expected to continue falling in the second half of 2016, down by 5.53 and 4.69% in the third and fourth quarter respectively. Owing to low prices of bulk commodities and RMB depreciation, import growth is expected to shrink by 6.65%. Nevertheless, as the process of cutting overcapacity accelerates and RMB depreciates further, the decline in import growth may not slow. Its growth is projected to continue to decline by 17.9% and 18.9% in the third and fourth quarter respectively. In 2016, the value of net exports is forecast to account for 1.25% of GDP.

Though the likelihood for the US to raise interest rates in the second half of 2016 had decreased, due to economic slowdown, RMB depreciation expectations and pressures of capital outflows still remain, suggesting that China is expected to deplete its foreign exchange reserves to stabilize RMB. China's foreign exchange reserves is projected to fall to 2.98 trillion dollars at the end of 2016.

In 2017, owing to the recovery of external market demand, such as the recovery of US economy, and RMB depreciating further, China's exports are expected to rebound. The exports growth is projected to go up by 1.65%. As the increase in exports of processing trade is expected to lead to the increase in imports of processing trade, the decline in imports is expected to slow significantly, imports growth is expected to be down by 5.87%. Foreign exchange reserves at the end of 2017 is projected to fall to 2.67 trillion dollars (see Fig. 2.6).

Table 2.1 Projected growth rates of foreign trade (%)

	Exports				Imports				Net exports as a share of GDP
	Constant price/RMB	Current price/US dollars	General trade at current price/US dollars	Processing trade at current price/US dollars	Constant price/RMB	Current price/US dollars	General trade at current price/US dollars	Processing trade at current price/US dollars	
2016	3.92	−6.01	−2.76	−12.22	3.97	−14.12	−13.85	−13.82	1.25
Q1	−0.31	−9.54	−7.33	−15.62	4.73	−13.07	−14.00	−17.51	0.87
Q2	5.34	−4.14	−0.99	−11.85	17.07	−6.65	−3.61	−15.17	1.35
Q3	5.02	−5.53	−1.42	−12.10	−0.43	−17.90	−19.42	−10.06	1.38
Q4	5.71	−4.69	−1.10	−9.17	−4.59	−18.90	−18.60	−12.34	1.39
2017	6.01	1.65	2.53	3.09	−1.74	−5.87	−10.04	4.27	1.14
Q1	8.20	3.91	5.19	5.23	2.57	−4.00	−8.89	6.64	0.95
Q2	3.05	−0.92	−0.61	2.20	−11.02	−13.18	−18.86	5.04	1.30
Q3	4.91	1.10	2.04	2.19	1.26	−1.81	−4.04	2.61	1.14
Q4	7.89	2.57	3.57	2.78	1.54	−3.47	−6.53	2.91	1.18

Source: CQMM team calculations

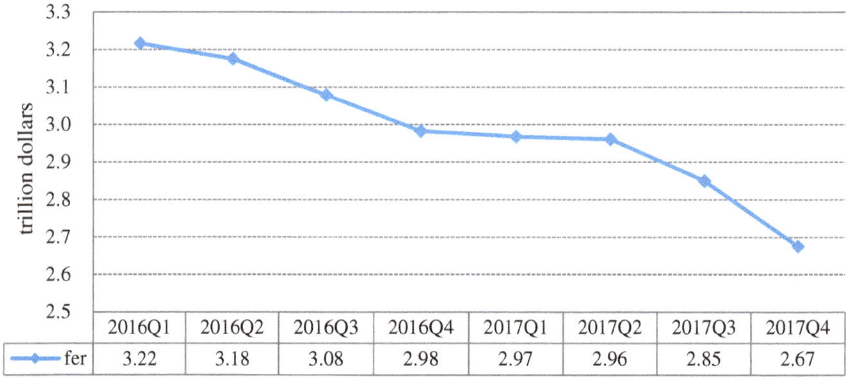

Fig. 2.6 Projected changes in foreign reserves. *Note* FER denotes foreign exchange reserves. *Source* CQMM team calculations

2.3.2 Growth Rates of Investment in Fixed Assets

In the second half of 2016, the excess capacity in manufacturing, the overstocking in real estate, and financial risks implied by high corporate leverage, will continue to curtail investment growth. Especially, the private investment growth is expected to slow down.

Growth of the FAI (excluding rural households) is forecast to expand by 9.72% in 2016, 0.47 percentage points lower than that in 2015. Its rate is expected to fall to 6.38% in 2017, 3.34 percentage points lower than that in 2016. Owing to the frenzied housing market, the total FAI picked up by 10.38% in the first quarter of 2016, but dropped to 8.13% in the second quarter. In the second half of 2016, the FAI is expected to be promoted by active fiscal policy. Its growth is projected to rise 10.26 and 10.11% in the third and fourth quarter respectively. Owing to downturn in property and shrinking of private investment, its growth rate in 2017 is expected to fluctuate around low levels, which reaches the highest of the whole year, say, 7.04%, in the second quarter.

The social FAI growth rate in 2016 is projected to stay at 8.97%, an increase of 0.84 percentage points over 2015. It is expected to fall to 6.51% in 2017. In terms of Source of funds, as shown by Table 2.2, the growth rate of FAI from state budget is forecast to maintain at 20.1% in 2016, and then slightly fall to 19.67% in 2017. The growth rate of FAI from domestic loans is expected to rebound to 14.87% in 2016, and then decline to 8.4%. The growth rate of FAI form self-funding is projected to reach 1.6% in 2016, and then climb to 2.02% in 2017. The growth rate of FAI from others is expected to rise to 39.93%, and then fall to 19.1% in 2017. In summary, due to the slowdown of manufacturing and private investment growth, the structure of Source of funds is expected to change, where the FAI from self-funding would drop dramatically, and those from others and domestic loans would expand slightly (see Fig. 2.7).

Table 2.2 Projected growth of total FAI by Source of funds (%)

	Total	State budget	Domestic loans	Self-raising funds	Others
2016	8.97	20.10	14.87	1.60	39.93
Q1	6.85	16.54	13.68	−0.01	31.33
Q2	8.86	24.63	11.64	2.28	41.86
Q3	9.32	20.95	12.98	2.60	41.70
Q4	10.69	18.48	21.38	1.49	43.93
2017	6.51	19.67	8.40	2.02	19.10
Q1	8.29	20.37	7.41	3.15	31.11
Q2	7.07	18.43	9.82	1.90	19.71
Q3	5.78	19.59	8.41	1.76	15.17
Q4	5.11	20.28	8.01	1.37	12.76

Source CQMM team calculations

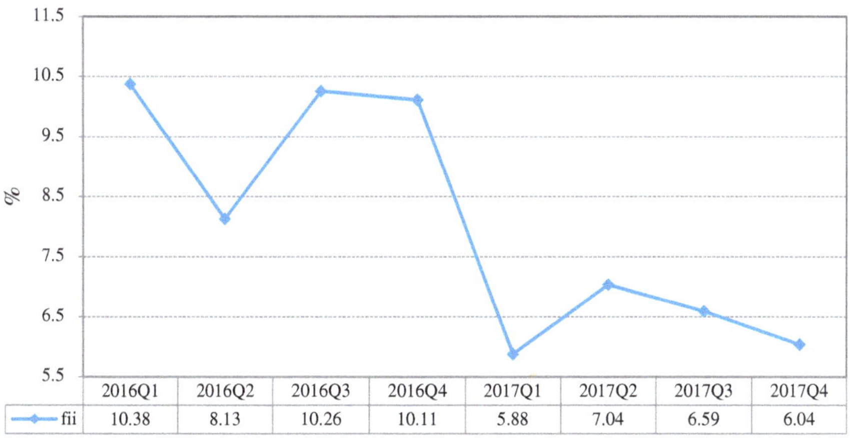

Fig. 2.7 Projected growth rates of FAI.YoY. *Note* fii denotes real FAI growth rates. *Source* CQMM team calculations

2.3.3 *Growth Rates of Consumption*

The economic downturn drags income growth down, and then curtail consumption growth. The household consumption is expected to edge down in the second half of 2016 and in 2017. The per capita real disposable income of urban households is projected to grow by 5.77% in 2016, down by 0.83 percentage points over 2015, and increase 5.43% in 2017, down further by 0.34 percentage points over 2016. The per capita real cash income of rural residents is expected to go up by 9.06% in 2016, 0.95 percentage points lower than that in 2015, and pick up by 8.29% in 2017, down further by 0.77 percentage points over 2016 (see Fig. 2.8).

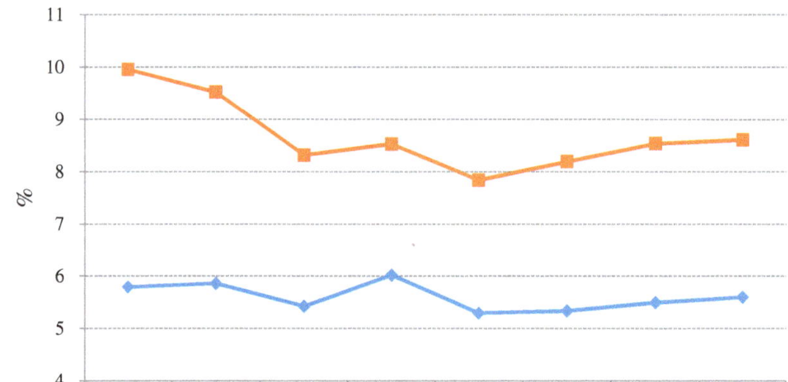

	2016Q1	2016Q2	2016Q3	2016Q4	2017Q1	2017Q2	2017Q3	2017Q4
yd_u_c_pc	5.79	5.86	5.42	6.02	5.30	5.33	5.49	5.60
yc_r_c_pc	9.95	9.52	8.31	8.52	7.83	8.19	8.53	8.60

Fig. 2.8 Projected growth rates of income of rural andurban households. YoY. *Note* yd_u_c_pc denotes per capita real disposable income of urban households, yc_r_c_pc denotes per capita real disposable income of rural residents. *Source* CQMM team calculations

Real household consumption is projected to grow by 8.06% in 2016, a decline of 0.04 percentage points over 2015, down further to 7.84% in 2017, 0.22 percentage points lower than that in 2016. Total retail sales of consumer goods at current price is expected to expanded by 10.3%, down slightly by 0.4 percentage points over 2015, and it is projected to fall slightly to 10.05%.

Real household consumption growth in 2016 is expected to appear before high after low tendency, down to 7.33% in the third quarter and 5.98% in the fourth quarter. Slightly fluctuate in 2017, with lowest rate of 7.08% in the third quarter. Growth of total retail sales of consumer goods at current price will stay stable in 2016, with the lowest rate of 9.94% in the third quarter. And it will maintain quite steady, with each quarter is expected to be above 10% (see Fig. 2.9).

In summary, according to the CQMM, China's economic growth is forecast to continue edging down due to decelerating investment growth and week exports growth, while the deflation risks remain low.

1. The GDP growth in 2016 is projected to rise 6.63%, 0.3 percentage points higher than that over 2015. The CPI is expected to climb 2.01%, an increase of 0.57 percentage points over 2015. The PPI is forecast to drop by 3.19%, 2.01 percentage points higher than that in 2015. And the GDP deflator is projected to pick up by 0.79%, an increase of 1.2 percentage points over 2015.
2. The decline in growth of manufacturing investment and private investment has put pressures on total investment growth. The growth of investment in fixed assets (excluding rural households) in 2016 is projected to expand by 9.72%, a drop of 0.47 percentage points over 2015.

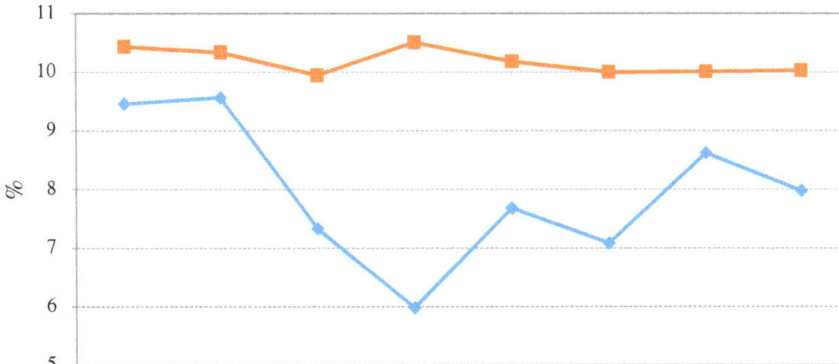

	2016Q1	2016Q2	2016Q3	2016Q4	2017Q1	2017Q2	2017Q3	2017Q4
CON_D_C	9.46	9.56	7.33	5.98	7.68	7.08	8.62	7.97
RETAIL	10.43	10.33	9.94	10.51	10.18	10.00	10.00	10.02

Fig. 2.9 Projected growth rates of consumption. YoY. *Note* CON_D_C denotes real household consumption growth rate; RETAIL denotes real growth rate of total retail sales of consumer goods. *Source* CQMM team calculations

3. The growth of per capita real disposable income of households is expected to edge down, suggesting that the household consumption is expected to slow down. The total retail sales of consumer goods in 2016 are forecast to go up by 10.3%, a decline of 0.4 percentage points over 2015.
4. Both the result of UK referendum and the lower-than-expected US GDP growth rate in the second quarter imply that the materialization of an important downside risk for advanced economies. The total value of exports in dollar terms in 2016 is expected to fall by 6.01%, down by 3.79 percentage points over 2015. The total value of imports is projected to decline by 14.12%, slightly up by 0.27 percentage points over 2015.
5. Owing to RMB depreciation expectations arising from economic slowdown and pressures put by capital outflows, China is projected to continue depleting its foreign exchange reserves to stabilize RMB. Foreign exchange reserves at the end of 2016 would fall to 2.98 trillion dollars.

Chapter 3
Policy Simulation: Macroeconomic Effects of Slowdown in Private Investment Growth

3.1 Background

In the first half of 2016, China's private investment growth dropped sharply, triggering concern and heated discussion among policymakers and scholars. Given the easing monetary policy implemented especially in the first quarter, what made the private investment growth plummet? Some clues may be found by analyzing changes in shares of private investment in total FAI by industry (see Table 3.1).

First, in the first half of 2016, impacted by the dramatic fall in the private investment growth, the ratio of private investment to total FAI declined to 61.46%, from 65.13% in the same period a year earlier, down by 3.67 percentage points. On a similar comparison, the ratio in the tertiary industry decreased from 30.43 to 28.39%, down by 2.04 percentage points, contributing 55.66% of the decline. The ratio in the secondary industry dropped from 32.60 to 30.77%, down by 1.83 percentage points, contributing 49.98% of the decline. And the ratio in the primary industry increased by 0.21 percentage points (see Table 3.1). Therefore, the decelerating investment growth in the second and tertiary industry is the key factor to explain the significant drop in the private investment growth.

Second, as to the secondary industry, the ratio of private investment to total FAI in production and supply of electricity, gas and water, did not fall but rise, from 1.62% up to 1.90%. As shown by Table 3.2, after 2012, the ratio kept rising steadily, suggesting that in the urban public infrastructure and services sectors, there is no evidence that the private investment has been crowded out, though the proportion of private investment is relatively small. In the first half of 2016, the key factor to explain the decline of the ratio in the secondary industry is the decelerating private investment growth in manufacturing and mining, where the former contributing 95.09% of the decline, and the latter contributing 17.43%. It is noteworthy that the decline of the ratio in mining did not first took place in the first half of 2016 but after 2012, though it is true that the decline has expanded since early 2016.

Center for Macroeconomic Research of Xiamen University,
China's Macroeconomic Outlook, Current Chinese Economic
Report Series, DOI 10.1007/978-981-10-3280-6_3

Table 3.1 Shares of private investment in total FAI by industry (%)

	Variables	Private investment	Primary industry	Secondary industry	Tertiary industry
2012H1	Proportion in total FAI	62.14	1.67	32.84	27.64
2013H1	Proportion in total FAI	63.74	1.61	32.69	29.44
	Change in proportion	1.60	−0.05	−0.15	1.80
	Contributions	100	−3.40	−9.31	112.67
2014H1	Proportion in total FAI	65.14	1.79	32.78	30.58
	Change in proportion	1.40	0.17	0.09	1.13
	Contributions	100	12.22	6.75	81.03
2015H1	Proportion in total FAI	65.12	2.11	32.60	30.43
	Change in proportion	−0.02	0.32	−0.19	−0.15
	Contributions	100	−1947.47	1126.77	920.69
2016H1	Proportion in total FAI	61.46	2.31	30.77	28.39
	Change in proportion	−3.66	0.21	−1.83	−2.04
	Contributions	100	−5.64	49.98	55.66

Source CQMM team calculations on CEIC data

Furthermore, in terms of subsectors of manufacturing, ratios of private investment to the FAI in non-metallic minerals, ferrous metals and non-ferrous metal smelting and pressing processing were down by 0.38, 0.04 and 0.14 percentage points respectively, in total contributing 32.59% of private investment growth in manufacturing. Ratios in general-purpose machinery and special-purpose machinery manufacturing fell rapidly as well, contributing 10.53 and 13.61% of the decline in private investment growth in manufacturing. As some of most valuable equipment has been installed in general-purpose machinery and special-purpose machinery manufacturing, such as mining, metallurgy, construction, metal processing, and so on, the decline of the ratios in these two sectors may also closely related to the private investment's exit from these sectors, besides, affected by the government's measures to constrain the capacity in these sectors (see Table 3.3).

Thirdly, as to the tertiary industry, the share of private investment in the FAI in transport, storage and post declined to 2.06% in the first half of 2016, from 2.20% in the same period last year, down by 0.14 percentage points, contributing 6.96% of

Table 3.2 Shares of private investment in the secondary industry by sector (%)

	Variables	Private investment in the secondary industry	Production and supply of electricity, gas and water	Construction	Mining	Manufacturing
2012H1	Proportion in total FAI	32.84	1.23	0.50	1.89	29.21
2013H1	Proportion in total FAI	32.69	1.30	0.40	1.74	29.34
	Change in proportion	−0.15	0.07	−0.10	−0.15	0.13
	Contributions	100	−49.61	68.18	100.72	−86.53
2014H1	Proportion in total FAI	32.78	1.36	0.44	1.58	29.50
	Change in proportion	0.09	0.06	0.04	−0.17	0.16
	Contributions	100	66.07	45.46	−175.54	170.21
2015H1	Proportion in total FAI	32.60	1.62	0.43	1.30	29.32
	Change in proportion	−0.19	0.26	−0.01	−0.27	−0.19
	Contributions	100	−140.87	4.52	147.84	101.23
2016H1	Proportion in total FAI	30.77	1.90	0.37	0.98	27.58
	Change in proportion	−1.83	0.27	−0.06	−0.32	−1.74
	Contributions	100	−14.86	3.43	17.43	95.09

Source CQMM team calculations on CEIC data

the decline. The share in water, conservancy, environment and public facilities only slightly declined by 0.01 percentage points, contributing 0.63 of the decline. The shares in education and health and social work, did not fall but rise, up by 0.03 and 0.04 percentage points respectively. The shares in culture, sports, and entertainment, together with public management, social securities, and social organizations, declined slightly as well, contributing very few to the decline (see Table 3.4). By contrast, the shares in these six sectors in the first half of 2015 were all up over those in the same period a year earlier. Nevertheless, the private investment in these sectors only accounts for 22.23% of the total in the tertiary industry, suggesting that changes in the private investment in these sectors are not the main factors to determine the changes in the tertiary industry. The main factors may lie behind the changes in other sectors in the tertiary industry.

As data on the private investment in other sectors in the tertiary industry are not available, we cannot find out which sectors are the main forces to determine the decline in private investment growth directly. However, the following evidence may be helpful.

Table 3.3 Shares of private investment in manufacturing by sector (%)

	Variables	Manufacturing	Nonmetallic minerals	Ferrous metal smelting and pressing processing industry	Non-ferrous metal smelting and pressing processing industry	General-purpose machinery	Special-purpose machinery	Automobile Manufacturing	Electrical machinery and equipment	Computer communi-cations and other electronic equipment
2012H1	Proportion in total FAI	29.21	3.17	1.06	0.96	2.09	2.03	1.58	2.06	0.97
2013H1	Proportion in total FAI	29.34	3.07	0.99	1.07	2.20	2.09	1.60	1.95	1.08
	Change in proportion	0.13	−0.10	−0.08	0.10	0.11	0.06	0.02	−0.11	0.11
	Contributions	100	−73.81	−60.92	80.67	85.74	42.73	16.79	−83.10	84.33
2014H1	Proportion in total FAI	29.50	3.04	0.81	1.02	2.30	2.07	1.59	1.97	1.02
	Change in proportion	0.16	−0.03	−0.18	−0.05	0.10	−0.02	−0.01	0.02	−0.06
	Contributions	100	−20.75	−111.77	−29.31	61.77	−10.80	−5.69	11.65	−38.63
2015H1	Proportion in total FAI	29.32	3.02	0.63	0.96	2.28	2.08	1.60	1.91	1.16
	Change in proportion	−0.19	−0.02	−0.18	−0.05	−0.02	0.02	0.01	−0.06	0.14
	Contributions	100	8.99	94.74	28.59	10.60	−8.82	−3.04	30.93	−75.70
2016H1	Proportion in total FAI	27.58	2.64	0.58	0.82	2.10	1.85	1.63	1.92	1.10
	Change in proportion	−1.74	−0.38	−0.04	−0.14	−0.18	−0.24	0.03	0.01	−0.06
	Contributions	100	21.74	2.56	8.29	10.53	13.61	−1.76	−0.72	3.51

Source CQMM team calculations on CEIC data

Table 3.4 Shares of private investment in the tertiary industry (%)

	Variables	Shares in private investment	Transport, storage and post	Water, conservancy, environment and public facilities	Education	Health and social work	Culture, sports, and entertainment	Public management, social securities, and social organizations
2012H1	Proportion in total FAI	27.64	1.58	1.64	0.30	0.17	0.53	0.51
2013H1	Proportion in total FAI	29.44	1.80	1.89	0.33	0.21	0.64	0.38
	Change in proportion	1.80	0.22	0.24	0.03	0.04	0.11	−0.13
	Contributions	100	11.95	13.53	1.88	2.10	6.13	−7.41
2014H1	Proportion in total FAI	30.58	1.97	2.20	0.38	0.24	0.69	0.37
	Change in proportion	1.13	0.17	0.31	0.04	0.03	0.05	−0.01
	Contributions	100	15.44	27.41	3.70	2.88	4.79	−0.78
2015H1	Proportion in total FAI	30.43	2.20	2.47	0.39	0.34	0.73	0.40
	Change in proportion	−0.15	0.23	0.28	0.02	0.10	0.04	0.03
	Contributions	100	−149.85	−182.68	−12.99	−65.89	−27.71	−18.70
2016H1	Proportion in total FAI	28.39	2.06	2.46	0.42	0.38	0.66	0.32
	Change in proportion	−2.04	−0.14	−0.01	0.03	0.04	−0.07	−0.08
	Contributions	100	6.96	0.63	−1.48	−1.90	3.41	3.73

Source CQMM team calculations on CEIC data

1. According to the *Classification of Sectors of China's National Economy* (GB/T 4754-2002), excluding the above mentioned six sectors, the rest of sectors in the tertiary industry are: wholesale and retail trades, information transmission, computer services and software, finance, real estate, leasing and business services, scientific research, technical services and geologic prospecting, and services to households and other services. It is some of these sectors that contributed 88.66% of changes in the decline of private investment growth in the tertiary industry in the first half of 2016.
2. Among the above mentioned seven sectors, wholesale and retail trades, together with the private investment in real estate, are two major sectors. Take real estate for example, the domestic investment in real estate development reached 8.66 trillion yuan in 2014, and investment from the state-owned and state holding enterprises (SOEs) and the collective-owned enterprises in total accounted for about 85% of the total, most of the rest was private investment.
3. In the first half of 2016, as the growth of the total retail sales of consumer goods stayed stable, the private investment in wholesale and retail trades would not change too much, suggesting that changes in the share of the private investment in real estate be the major determinant to the decline of private investment growth in the tertiary industry. As shown by Fig. 3.1, in June, 2015, for real estate development, the growth rate of the investment from the SOEs went up sharply from 2.7% at the end of 2015 to 17.0% in January, 2016, overtaking that from the total FAI for the first time, while in the same period the rate of property investment only slightly rose from 1.0 to 3.0%, suggesting that the relatively lower growth rate of the investment from non-SOEs dragged down that of total investment. On account of this, the share of investment from SOEs rose from 15.0% at the end of 2015 to 16.6% in June, 2016, 2.0 percentage points higher than that in the same period a year earlier.

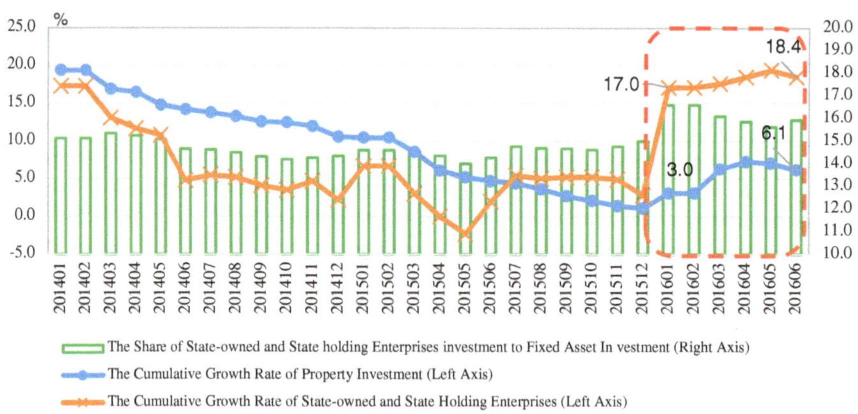

Fig. 3.1 Growth rates of property investment from SOEs. *Source* CQMM team calculations on CEIC data

Furthermore, in terms of incremental funds in the real estate development, in the first half of 2015, the investment increased by 193.6 billion yuan over the same period a year earlier, and the share of investment from SOEs was only 6.01%. By contrast, in the first half of 2016, the investment increased by 267.6 billion yuan over the same period last year, and the investment from SOEs grew by 115.4 billion yuan, accounting for 43.1% of the total increment.

In summary, the dramatic drop in the share of private investment in total FAI is attributable to the following two direct causes:

First, the private capital accelerated to exit from those manufacturing sectors with overcapacity, and in the meantime, due to technology barrier, shortage of funds, or entry barrier, the private capital was not able to enter into some high-end manufacturing sectors and some quasi-public services, leading to decelerating growth of private investment. These exiting funds turn to invest in the fictitious economy, such as commodity futures, housing markets in upper-tier cities, dollars markets, gold markets, and so on. In addition, some of them outflew, making the growth rate of OFDI accelerated significantly in the first half of 2016.

Second, the growth rate of private investment in real estate in the first half of 2016 did not rise significantly, dragging down its share in real estate investment, while the share of the SOEs' investment climbed correspondingly. One cause is that, owing to the bank credit preference and the relatively high fund entry barrier, private capital, which endowed with limited funds and other resources, didn't have the capability for competing with the SOEs in upper-tier cities, making incremental private investment really limited. The other cause is that most private capital was concentrated in lower-tier cities, where the property market is facing the pressure from destocking, making private capital reluctant to increase investment. Therefore, the fact that the private investment growth dropped dramatically in the first half of 2016 reflects the serious regional divergence of real estate. During the period that property boom in upper-tier cities coexisting with great pressure of destocking in lower-tier cities, it is hard for private capital to challenge the SOEs.

3.2 Further Research

The above analysis suggests that the slowdown of private investment growth is closely related to current supply-side structural reform. On one side, the action to cut overcapacity accelerated, making private investment exit from the relevant sectors. On the other side, during the period that property boom in upper-tier cities coexisting with great pressure of destocking in lower-tier cities, private capital was crowded out by more powerful SOEs. All these reflect that there are at least two weaknesses in current supply-side structural reform. The first is that the measures taken so for to curb overcapacity emphasized too much on the quantity but not the quality. And the result is that, though some excess capacity had been cut, it is difficult for the exiting capital to enter into some more profitable real economy. The second is that the measures to cut overcapacity cannot eliminate those real zombie enterprises by market mechanism, but by government mandates, the latter discarding as useless some more productive capacity owned by private enterprises. Furthermore, the market mechanism does not work well even in those competitive markets. The SOEs, with their credit endorsed by the government, are always easier than private businesses to enter into the capital markets, resulting in virtually unfair competition. And thus, in order to increase effective investment while curbing excess capacity, it is necessary to make some adjustment on the current reform.

In our opinion, the keys to the supply-side reform include: return to the markets, increase the returns on investment (ROI), and stimulate investment and allocate resources according to the market.

Actually, the slowdown of private investment growth is not a new problem which occurred this year. Since 2012, the year in which statistical data on private investment for the first time released, the private investment growth has kept decelerating, owing to the decline of ROI in real economy. The ROI in the first and second quarter of 2016 continued this downward trend, but no sudden fall took place (see Fig. 3.2).

The ROI is an indicator that reflects business operation efficiency comprehensively. There are many factors that affect the ROI, including Assets, liabilities, the gross profit, the corporate income tax, and so on. As Assets, liabilities, and the gross profit, are all determined by businesses, the only factor that the government is able to determine directly is the taxation system. China's current taxation structure takes the indirect tax, such as value-added tax (VAT) and consumption tax, as the main body. Such structure is not help for business operation and reinvestment, especially during economic recession. When the goods market is not clearing, it is hard for business to shift the tax burden to consumers at the low stream, making businesses

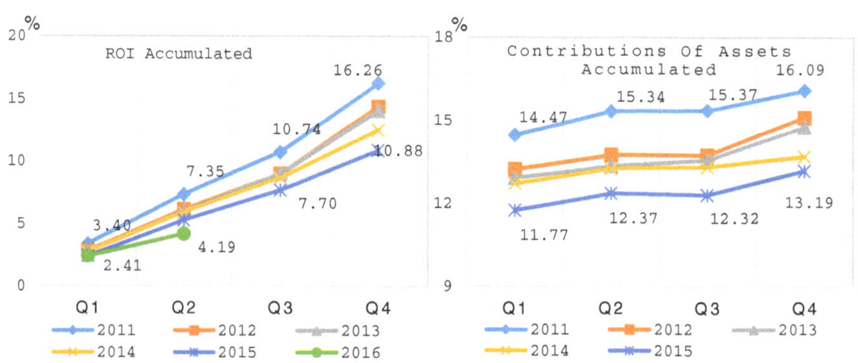

Fig. 3.2 ROI of industrial enterprises. *Note* (1) ROI = (gross profit − income tax)/(total assets − total liabilities) = (gross profit × 0.75)/(total assets − total liabilities). (2) Data are seasonally adjusted. *Source* CQMM team calculations on CEIC data

have to bear much of the operating tax burden. Besides, much of fees and charges in the social insurance system are mostly put on the businesses. And the result is, the worse is the economy, the greater are the tax burden and cost pressure put on businesses. From this perspective, we suggest that, during economic slowdown, in order to improve their ROI, the government should help businesses reduce their costs and burdens by tax cut and fees and charges reduction. And this would be an effective approach to solving the problem of decelerating investment growth, especially the problem of dramatic drop in private investment growth.

In the next section, the CQMM is used to evaluate the macroeconomic effects of improvement on the ROI.

3.3 Policy Simulation

3.3.1 Model Specification Adjustment

In order to simulate effects of improvement on the ROI, the original CQMM was made some adjustments. The major adjustments are mentioned as follows:

First, equations in the investment module are revised. The investment equation in the original model was specified by the FAI from various sources of funds, not including the FAI from private and non-private investment. In the new equation, the FAI are classified as the private investment and the SOEs' investment to explain gross capital formation and GDP. As current statistical data based on surveys can only be used to measure the ROI of industrial enterprises, we introduced the variable of private investment in industrial sectors as the intermediate indicator of variable of private investment. In addition, in order to distinguish the private investment and the SOEs' investment, we assume that the ROI of industrial enterprises can only affect the private investment in industrial sectors, but cannot affect the SOEs' investment (see Fig. 3.3).

Secondly, for convenience, the ROI variable is assumed as exogenous, its conduction route is mainly via tax adjustment, including the decline of taxes less subsidies on production and imports, and the decrease of income tax. It is noteworthy that the tax adjustment usually has endogenous effects on different modules of the model. For we have studied the effects of tax adjustment in the previous report based on CQMM, it is reduced to exogenous changes on this report.

3.3.2 Simulation Scenarios Planning

Based on the estimated ROI of industrial enterprises, two scenarios are designed as follows:

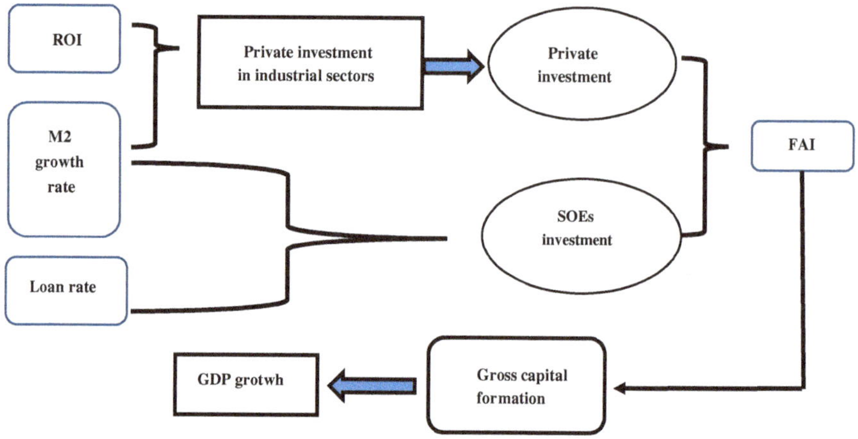

Fig. 3.3 Conduction route of the ROI on private investment

In *Scenario 1*, the ROI of industrial enterprises in 2014, 2015, and the first half year of 2016 are kept same as that in the same period of 2013.[1] The aim of this scenario simulation is to evaluate the effects of improvement of ROI on major macroeconomic variables.

In *Scenario 2*, the situation becomes worse. The ROI of industrial enterprises dropped sharply in 2014, just as in 2015. In 2015 and 2016 they are kept same as that in 2014. The aim of this scenario simulation is to evaluate the macroeconomic effects of continued decline of ROI.

Detailed differences are shown by Fig. 3.4.

3.3.3 *Simulation Results*

3.3.3.1 Results of Comparing Scenario 1 with Baseline

First, the increase of ROI would accelerate private investment growth and increase the share of private investment in the FAI. As shown by Fig. 3.5, affected by the increase of ROI, the private investment growth rates after 2015 in *Scenario 1* would be 5.0 percentage points higher than that in the baseline simulation (hereafter *Baseline*) per quarter on average. In the meantime, they would increase quarter on quarter, quite different from the situation in *Baseline* that they decline steadily. Furthermore, shares of private investment in total FAI would increase significantly,

[1]From Fig. 3.4, we can find that the turning point of ROI, on which the baseline model estimation is based, showed up in 2013. On account of this, we assume that the ROI in 2013 is maintain in 2014, 2015, and the first half of 2016.

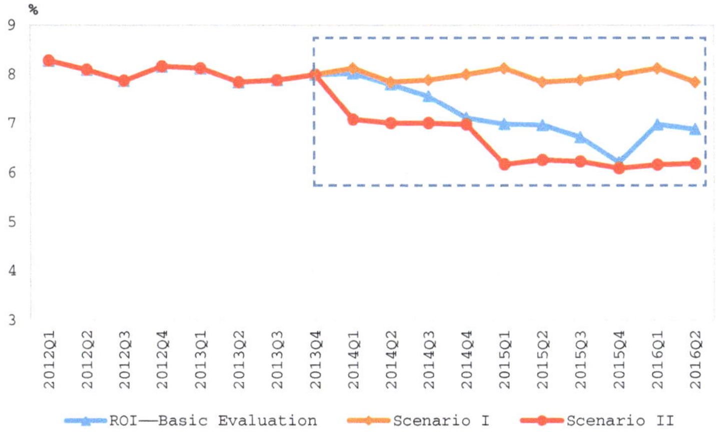

Fig. 3.4 The ROI simulation and scenario simulation. *Note* (1) ROI = (gross profit − income tax)/(total assets − total liabilities) = (gross profit × 0.75)/(total assets − total liabilities). (2) Data are seasonally adjusted. *Source* CQMM team calculations on CEIC data

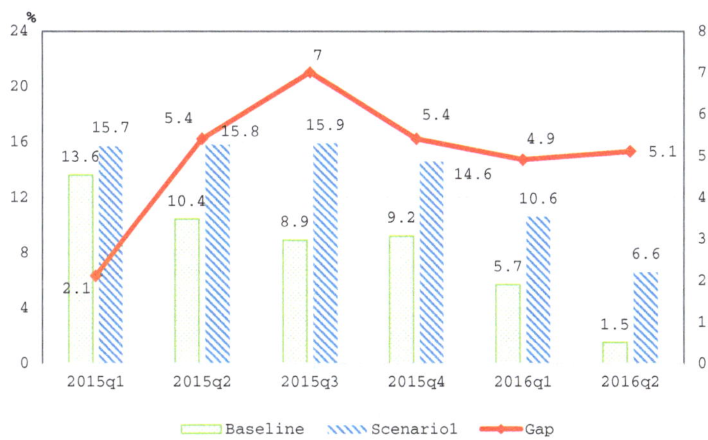

Fig. 3.5 Changes in private investment growth rates (*Scenario 1*). *Note* (1) *Baseline* denotes results of the baseline simulation. To make simulation results closer to real economy, equations concerning major endogenous variables have been adjusted by additional factor approach. (2) *Scenario 1* denotes the simulation results of *Scenario 1*. (3) Gap = *Scenario 1*-Baseline. *Source* CQMM team calculations on CEIC data

and the increasing range would expand vibrantly. In the second quarter of 2016, the share in *Scenario 1* would be 2.10 percentage points higher than that in *Baseline* (see Fig. 3.6).

Secondly, the pickup in growth rates of private investment would accelerate the GDP growth. As shown by Fig. 3.7, the GDP growth rates in *Scenario 1* would be 0.94 percentage points higher than those in baseline simulation per quarter on

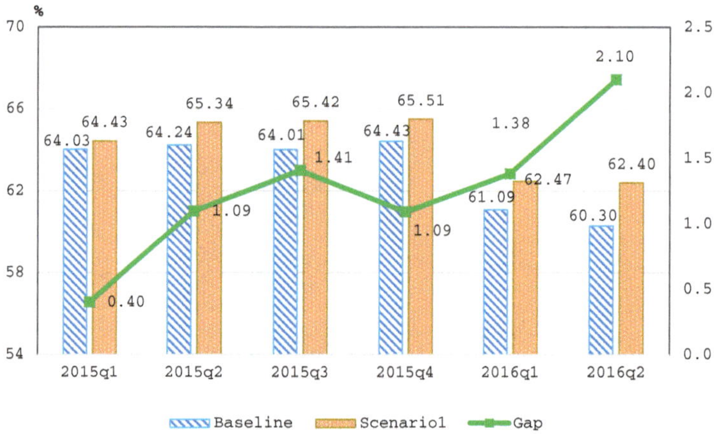

Fig. 3.6 Changes in shares of private investment in the FAI (*Scenario 1*). *Note* (1) *Baseline* denotes results of the baseline simulation. To make simulation results closer to real economy, equations concerning major endogenous variables have been adjusted by additional factor approach. (2) *Scenario 1* denotes the simulation results of *Scenario 1*. (3) Gap = *Scenario 1-Baseline*. *Source* CQMM team calculations on CEIC data

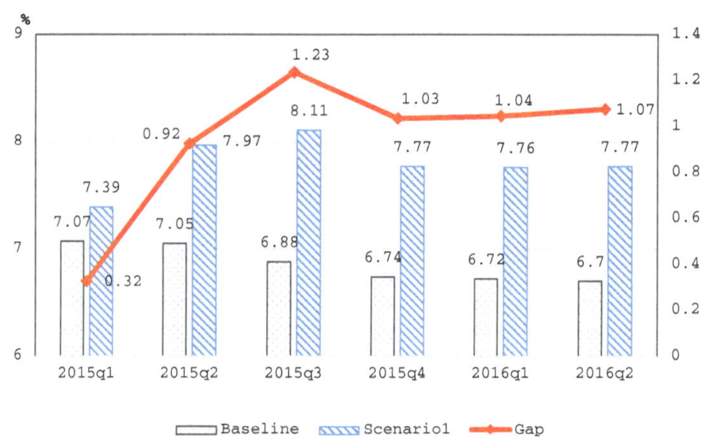

Fig. 3.7 Changes in GPD growth rates (Scenario 1). *Note* (1) *Baseline* denotes results of the baseline simulation. To make simulation results closer to real economy, equations concerning major endogenous variables have been adjusted by additional factor approach. (2) *Scenario 1* denotes the simulation results of *Scenario 1*. (3) Gap = *Scenario 1-Baseline*. *Source* CQMM team calculations on CEIC data

average. In 2015 and the first half of 2016, the GDP growth rates would maintain approximately between 7.7 and 7.8%, 0.8–1.2% points higher than the present growth rates, almost same as those in 2012 and 2013.

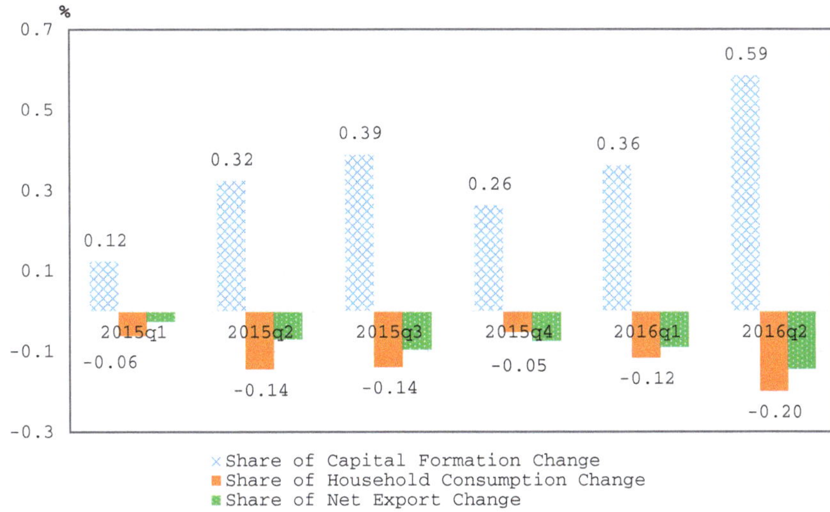

Fig. 3.8 Changes in aggregate demand structure (*Scenario 1*). *Source* CQMM team calculations on CEIC data

Thirdly, as to the aggregate demand structure, affected by the increase of the FAI growth rate, the share of gross capital formation in GDP would rise, and the share of household consumption and net exports in GDP would decline slightly. As shown by Fig. 3.8, in the second quarter of 2016, the share of gross capital formation in Scenario 1 would be 0.59 percentage points higher than that in *Baseline*, owing to the growth rate of household consumption lower than that of investment. And the share of household consumption would fall by 0.20 percentage points, due to the accelerating GDP growth. The growth rate of household consumption would also be higher than that in *Baseline*. In addition, the share of net exports would go down, owing to the increase of imports growth rate when the domestic demand goes up.

3.3.3.2 Results of Comparing Scenario 2 with Baseline

Firstly, based on the assumption that the ROI drop sharply a year ahead, the private investment growth rates in *Scenario 2* would be 3.30 percentage points lower than that in *Baseline* per quarter on average. In 2016, due to the tail effects of the 2015 base, its rate would be almost same as that in *Baseline*. In the meantime, shares of private investment in total FAI would drop significantly. In 2015, the share in *Scenario 2* would be 0.68 percentage points lower than that in *Baseline* per quarter on average, and down by 0.57 and 0.14 percentage points than those in the first and second quarter of 2016 respectively (see Figs. 3.9 and 3.10).

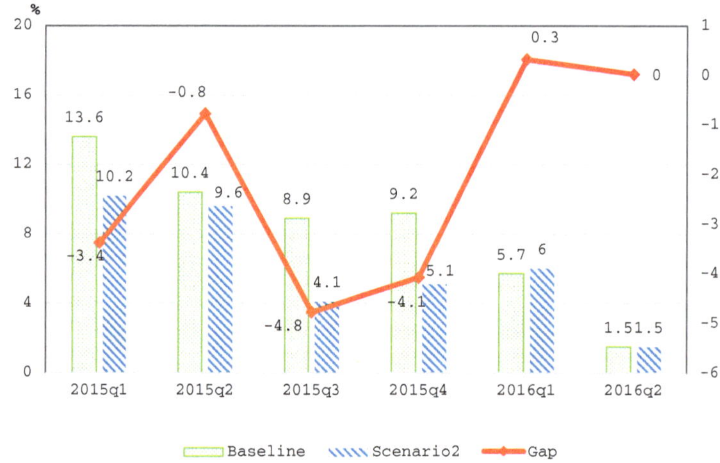

Fig. 3.9 Changes in private investment growth rates (*Scenario 2*). *Note* (1) *Baseline* denotes results of the baseline simulation. To make simulation results closer to real economy, equations concerning major endogenous variables have been adjusted by additional factor approach. (2) *Scenario 2* denotes the simulation results of *Scenario 2*. (3) Gap = *Scenario 2-Baseline*. *Source* CQMM team calculations

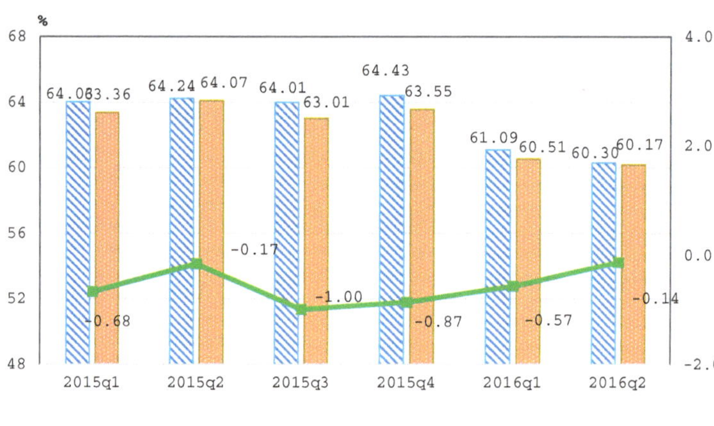

Fig. 3.10 Changes in shares of private investment in the FAI (*Scenario 2*). *Note* (1) *Baseline* denotes results of the baseline simulation. To make simulation results closer to real economy, equations concerning major endogenous variables have been adjusted by additional factor approach. (2) *Scenario 2* denotes the simulation results of *Scenario 2*. (3) Gap = *Scenario 2-Baseline*. *Source* CQMM team calculations

Second, the decline in growth rates of private investment would decelerate the GDP growth. As shown by Fig. 3.11, the GDP growth rates in *Scenario 1* would be 0.42 percentage points lower than those in *Baseline* per quarter on average,

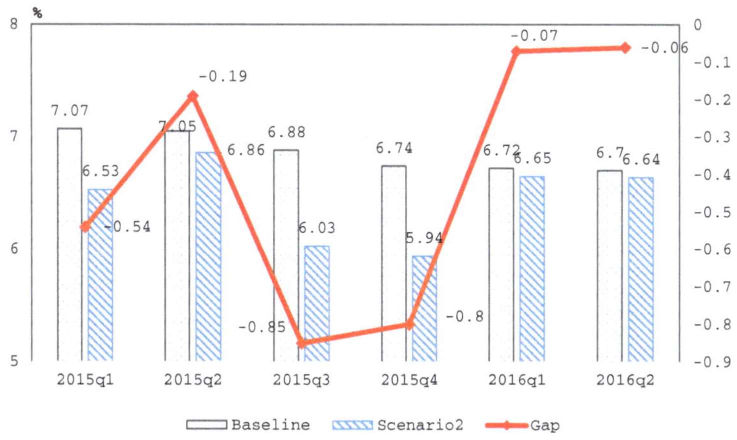

Fig. 3.11 Changes in GPD growth rates (*Scenario 2*). *Note* (1) *Baseline* denotes results of the baseline simulation. To make simulation results closer to real economy, equations concerning major endogenous variables have been adjusted by additional factor approach. (2) *Scenario 2* denotes the simulation results of *Scenario 2*. (3) Gap = *Scenario 2-Baseline*. *Source* CQMM team calculations

suggesting that the GDP growth rate in 2015 would fall to 6.5%, and would further decelerate to 6.3%, down by 0.4 percentage points than the current GDP growth rate.

Thirdly, as to the aggregate demand structure, the share of gross capital formation in GDP would fall, and the share of household consumption would rise, due to the increase of its growth rate lower than that of investment growth. However, the growth rate of consumption would be lower than that in *Baseline*, in that GDP growth decelerated. In addition, the share of net exports would rise, for the decline of imports growth rate after the domestic demand would go down (Fig. 3.12).

In summary, the results of the above two scenario simulations indicate:

1. The increase of ROI would accelerate the private investment and GDP growth. Besides, if the ROI stay at about 8%, the increase of private investment growth would make the GDP growth rate kept between 7 and 8%, which is the goal that China's macroeconomic policy tried to achieve in the past several years. Though the rise of private investment growth rate would increase the shares of investment in aggregate demand structure, it would not constrain household consumption growth, but instead increase the household consumption via accelerating economic growth.
2. The continued decline in the ROI would decrease the private investment and GDP growth. It is noteworthy that when ROI fall to some extent, the decline in private investment growth would make the GDP growth decelerate to below 6.5%, what is the bottom line set by the government.

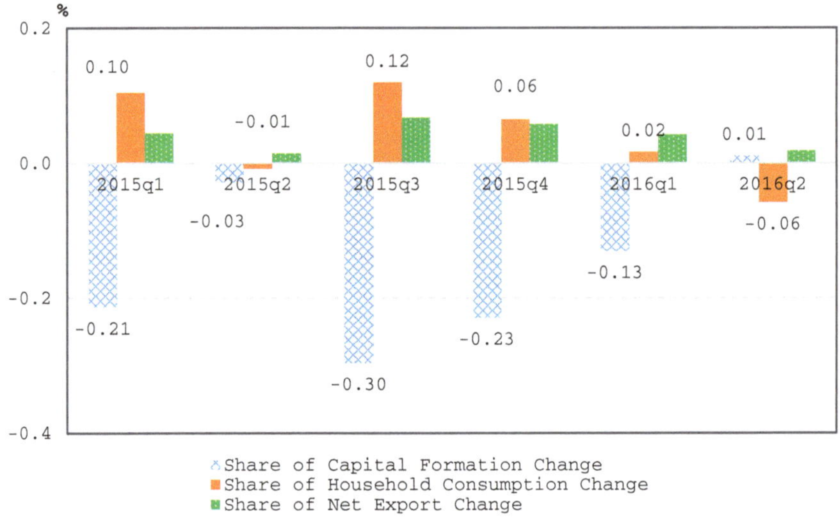

Fig. 3.12 Changes in Aggregate Demand Structure (*Scenario 2*). *Source* CQMM team calculations

In conclusion, in the first half of 2016, the contribution of gross capital formation to economic growth rate was 37.0%, only slightly down by 0.6 percentage points over the same period last year. It is the rapid growth of infrastructure investment and property investment that offset the decline in manufacturing investment growth. However, the investment growth supported by both infrastructure and real estate investment would not maintain in the second half of 2016. We find that whether the decline in the FAI growth rate would be reversed depends on whether the manufacturing investment decelerating growth, which accounts for about one third of total FAI, would stop falling and resume to rise. Policy simulation results in this section show that the increase of private investment growth rests on the rise of ROI.

Chapter 4
Policy Implications and Suggestions

That the private investment growth dropped dramatically is one of most significant macroeconomic events in 2016. As we know, private economy has grown up to be the main body of China's economy. Today's private enterprises contribute over 60% of GDP, over 80% of employment, and over half of tax revenues. Private investment accounts for over 60% of total FAI, and over 85% of manufacturing investment. The efficiency of private investment[1] is always higher than that of state capital investment as well. Policy simulation in this report shows that if the ROI would be increased to about 8%, which maintained in 2013, then the share of private investment would be raise significantly, and that would make China maintain its growth rate at about 7–8%. Conversely, if there would be a sharp fall of ROI, then the private investment would correspondingly drop dramatically, which would make China's economic growth rate drop below its present level. Thus, the results of policy simulation verify that China's economy cannot suffer a sharp fall in private investment growth, whatever in the near term or in the long term.

Our studies find that, owing to the global rebalancing and the domestic structural transformation, the private investment growth continued slowing down since 2011. Nevertheless, the sudden drop of its growth since early 2016 is largely attributable to China's current implementation of supply front structural reform. Therefore, we suggest that, in the short run, the demand-side measures to stabilize economic growth should be continued in order to resume private entrepreneurs' expectations on China's economic outlook, while in the long run, institutional reforms needed by the supply-side structural reforms should be made.

The policy suggestions are presented as follows:

1. Implement neutral monetary policy to stabilize economic growth. The relatively loose monetary policy in the first of 2016, play an active role in stabilizing China's economic growth, but to some extent should be responsible for the

[1]The efficiency of investment is measured by the investment multiplier, that is, the ratio of incremental investment to incremental GDP.

Center for Macroeconomic Research of Xiamen University,
China's Macroeconomic Outlook, Current Chinese Economic
Report Series, DOI 10.1007/978-981-10-3280-6_4

property boom in the upper-tier cities. Therefore, the monetary policy in the second of 2016 should return to be neutral, guiding the bank credit to enter into the real economy and help it recover, while in the meantime reining financial Assets bubbles. As GDP growth of US and the euro area so far lower than expected, and the US Federal Reserves to postpone raising interest rates, the external environment for China to reduce interest rates has been relieved, while the economic downside pressures are still strong. We suggest that the central bank cut interest rates and the reserve requirement ratios in the second half of 2016, which will help boost the economy by reducing business costs, relieving the possible impacts of debt default, and promoting exports.

2. Carry out expansionary fiscal policy to lift China's economic growth. The recovery of private investment is up to the resuming of private businesses' expectations on China economic outlook. Before the positive effects of supply-side structural reform play, the near-term task of stabilizing growth relies on demand-side management measures. Given that the monetary policy returns to be neutral, the fiscal policy should play major role. In the first half of 2016, the fiscal deficit amounted to 365.61 billion yuan, meaning that there is still 1.8 trillion-yuan deficit room in second half of 2016. As the infrastructure investment has such features as with big volume, long construction period, high risks, and low ROI, it is often taken by the government. Instead of crowding out private investment, the infrastructure investment is often helpful to attract private investment. Therefore, it would be the main field that loose fiscal policy can participate in. Furthermore, as expenditures on people's livelihood, such as public health insurance, education, government-subsidized housing units, and so on, can stimulate household consumption directly via increasing household disposable income, they are also the focus of fiscal expenditure policy.
   In terms of fiscal revenues, as tax reform is always closely related to complex interests of groups and takes time, in the near term, the feasible approach is to make some minor changes in current policies within the established framework of tax law. For example, as to the reform of replacing business tax with VAT on May 1, 2016, the government need to detail the rules to realize its goal to relieve business tax burden, especially for those private enterprises.
3. Lower market entry barriers and stabilize businesses' expectations for private investment. At the stage of demand structural transformation, the capital tends to exit from sunset industries and overcapacity sectors and then enter into sunrise industries and newly-emerging demand sectors. Such a tendency is helpful for promoting investment and supply-side structural transformation. Since 2010, China's services have grown rapidly. However, further development of the services industry is being stalled by commonly existing monopoly, regulation, and ownership discrimination. Thus, it is urgent for the government to clean up these barriers and encourage equal competition. In the meantime, it is also necessary to open new investment fields, lower investment costs, and improve the ROI of private capital.

4. Take measures to support private financing. As we know, small and micro businesses are finding it difficult and costly to obtain financing. The government has made great efforts to address this problem, but such a problem stays unsolved, and it seems to become more serious recently. To address this situation, the government should take measures to help provide financial services to private businesses, provide credit consulting service and information service for private businesses, and establish medium and small financial institutions sponsored by private capital, and so on, in order to expand financing channels for private businesses.
   China's current financial institutions are mainly state-owned and monopolistic, determining that private businesses' financing problem is hard to solve. If freer, more open, and more competitive financial institutions can be established, then the problem of information asymmetry between borrowers and lenders can be solved very well. Thus, the problem of high financing cost faced by private businesses may be alleviated. In addition, establishing multi-level capital markets by strengthening supervision on China's securities markets, in order to open a more convenient financing channel for private businesses, is also a long-term approach to address the problem.
5. Make reforms on taxation structure to relieve business tax burden. The cost reduction task, as one of measures in the context of supply-side structural reform, should be taken on not only by the businesses through technological innovation and management improvement, but by the government through tax cuts and reduction in fees and charges.

For business taxpayers, the indirect tax, which includes VAT, consumption tax, and business tax, accounts for 55% of total tax, together with corporate income tax, which accounts for 20% of total tax, meaning that over 75% of total tax are paid by businesses. Though most of these taxes' burden will pass on to low-stream consumers by tax shift, especially those indirect taxes. But the heavy statutory tax is shown by higher commodity prices, impairing their international competitiveness. From the perspective of income distribution, the indirect tax is regressive, meaning that richer taxpayers bear less tax burden while poorer taxpayers bear more. And thus, the indirect tax exacerbates inequality and has negative impacts on household consumption. Taking into account social insurance contribution, high financing cost, and various government fees and charges, business operation costs are very high. That would be the cause that some private enterprises exit from real economy then enter into felicitous economy, or bring about accelerating growth of capital outflows and the OFDI.

In summary, on its road to establish modern public finance, China should not only continue to clean up unnecessary and/or unreasonable charges and fees, but put more emphasis on changing its current tax system centered on the indirect tax to a new one centered on the direct tax as the main body. To be specific, the government should both reduce the current rates of VAT and consumption tax, and try to levy possession property tax, estate and gift tax, and adopt comprehensive personal tax system, in order to reduce businesses' tax burden and let these direct taxes perform their functions in income redistribution, so as to stimulate household consumption demand. As a result, whatever on the supply side or on the demand side, these measures would have positive effects on the increase of private investment growth.

Appendix
Report on the Questionnaire Survey on China's Macroeconomic Situation and Policy in 2016

August 2016, No.7.

To keep abreast of China's macroeconomic situation and policy, a semiannual questionnaire survey has been launched since August 2013, jointly sponsored by the Economic Information Daily, which is an affiliate to China's Xinhua News Agency, and the Center for Macroeconomic Research at Xiamen University, which is one of the Key Research Institutes of Humanities and Social Sciences of the Ministry of Education of China.

In this 7th questionnaire survey, twenty-one questions about China's macroeconomic situation and policy have been raised. Many distinguished economists in relevant fields are invited to join this survey by email in late July, 2016. We finally got responses from 116 of them. This survey reflects the latest understandings and judgments of these experts concerning the global economic situations, forecasts of some major indicators about China's macro-economy, China's macroeconomic policies to be implemented in the second half of 2016, and predictions of China's average economic growth rate during the 13th Five Year Plan (2016–20).

Detailed results of the survey are presented as follows:

1. **The global economic situations in 2016**

According to the latest economic forecast by the IMF on June 23, the US GDP growth rate is projected to be 2.2% in 2016. Hence, a question is raised on the trend of US economic growth. The result is that, 58% of the experts forecast that the US GDP growth rate in 2016 would be "between 2.0 and 2.2%", 30% predict that it would be "between 2.3 and 2.5%", 10% expected that it would be "below 1.9%", 1% forecast that it would be "between 2.6 and 2.8%", and 1% predict that it would be "2.9% or more". In sum, more than two thirds of the experts forecast that the US economic growth would slow down in 2016, while more than 30% of the experts predict that the US economy would rebound in 2016, more optimistic than that of IMF's forecast.

Impacted by the outcome of UK referendum, the forecast of GDP growth rate of the euro area was revised down to 1.6 in 2016 and 1.4% in 2017 by the IMF on July 8. The result of survey on the trend of the euro area's economic growth is that, 83% of the experts predict that the euro area GDP growth rate would be "between 1.3 and

Center for Macroeconomic Research of Xiamen University,
China's Macroeconomic Outlook, Current Chinese Economic
Report Series, DOI 10.1007/978-981-10-3280-6

1.6%" in 2016, 9% forecast that it would be "between 1.7 and 2.0%", 8% expect that it would be "below 1.2%", and no experts chose "between 2.1 and 2.4%" or "2.5% or more". In sum, more than 90% of the experts predict that the economy of the euro area would show a downward trend in 2016. But nearly 10% of them believed that the euro area economy would recover in 2016.

In the first half of 2016, the global and domestic bulk commodity markets recovered and the prices of bulk commodity went up significantly. What is the trend in the second half of 2016? The survey shows that, 59% of the experts forecast that the global commodity prices in the second half of 2016 will be volatile, 29% predict that it would rise, 2% expect that it would decline steadily. In sum, more than 30% of the experts believed that the commodity prices in the second half of 2016 would show an upward trend.

Brexit may trigger deflation in the euro area. What is the trend of the exchange rate of the EURO against the USD in the second half of 2016? The survey shows that, 77% of the experts predict that it would be "slightly depreciated". 14% claim that it would be "volatile", 6% forecast that it would be "slightly revaluated", while 3% expect that it would be "significantly depreciated", and no one anticipate that it would be "significantly revaluated". In sum, more than three quarters of the experts predict that there would be a continuous trend of depreciation of the EURO against the USD in the second half of 2016.

2. **Forecast of China's major macroeconomic indicators in 2016**

According to the data released by China National Bureau of Statistics (NBS) on July 15, China's GDP increased by 6.7% in the first half of 2016. What is the growth rate of China's GDP in 2016? The survey shows that, 59% of the experts predict that it would be "between 6.5 and 6.7%", 20% forecast that it would be "between 6.4 and 6.5%", 19% expect that it would be "between 6.7 and 6.9%", 1% choose "7.0% or more" and 1% choose "6.3% or less". In sum, 80% of the experts predict that China's economic growth would continue to edge down in 2016.

China's CPI increased by 2.1% in the first half of 2016. What is the trend of China's CPI in 2016? The survey shows that, 61% of the experts predict that it would be "between 2.1 and 2.5%", 31% forecast that it would be "between 1.6 and 2.0%", 6% expect that it would be "between 2.6 and 3.0%", 1% anticipate that it would be "1.5% or less", and 1% expect it would be "3.1% or more". In sum, more than two thirds of the experts expect that the CPI growth rate would rise in the second half of 2016, while more than 30% predict that it would continue to decline.

China's PPI decreased by 3.9% in the first half of 2016. What is the trend of the PPI in 2016? The survey shows that, 67% of the experts expect it to be "between −3.8 and −2.8%", 15% predict t that it would be "between −2.7 and −1.7%", 14% hold the view that it would be "−3.9% or less", 3% expect that it would be "between −1.6 and −0.6%", and 1% claim that it would be "−0.5% or more". In sum, 86% of the experts predict that the decline in China's PPI would be slowed in 2016.

By June 30, 2016, the rate of the US dollar against RMB was about 6.6312. What is the trend of the RMB exchange rate in 2016? The survey shows that, 44% of the experts predict that it would be "between 6.6 and 6.7%", 32% expect that it would be "between 6.7 and 6.8%", 19% forecast that it would be "between 6.5 and 6.6%", 3% claim that it would be "6.9% or more", and 2% think that it would be "6.4 or less". In sum, more than 30% of the experts forecast a continued depreciation of the RMB exchange rate in 2016. But more than 20% of the experts expect that the RMB exchange rate would appreciate, and more than 40% forecast that it would maintain stable.

The CFETS slightly depreciated in the first half of 2016. On June 30, the CFETS devalued by 5.86% from last year. What is the trend of CFETS in the second half of 2016? We also conducted a questionnaire survey about this. The survey showed that 51% of the experts expected it would be "depreciate slower and lower than 5.86%". 27% considered that it would be "continue to depreciate and higher than 5.86%". 20% of the experts thought that "keep steady at an appropriate and balanced level". 2% claimed that it would be "slight revaluation". In sum, nearly 90% of the experts believed a continuous trend of depreciation of CFETS in the second half of 2016.

China's investment in fixed assets (excluding rural households) in the first half of 2016 was about 25.84 trillion yuan, up by 9.0% YoY, 1.7 percentage points lower than that in the first quarter. What is the growth rate of China's investment in fixed assets in 2016? The survey shows that, 50% of the experts expect that the growth rate of total investment would be "between 8.1 and 9.0%", 40% think that it would be "between 9.1 and 10.0%". 5% forecast that it would be "between 10.1 and 11.0%". 3% expect that it would be "8.0% or less", and 2% claim that it would be "11.1% or more". In sum, more than 50% of the experts predict that total investment growth would slow down in the second half of 2016., and 47% predict that it would continue rising.

In the first half of 2016, China's investment in real estate market was 4.66 trillion yuan, up by 6.1% YoY, slightly down by 0.1% over that in the first quarter. What is the impact of property investment on private investment? The survey shows that, 61% of the experts expect that it would be "negative and the real estate expansion increased the cost of land and capital, thus reduced private investment". 30% think that it would be "positive and it can stimulate private investment and provide new opportunities", and 9% claim that there would be "no impact". In sum, more than 60% of the experts believe that the expansion of property investment reduced private investment in China.

China's private investment growth dropped sharply to 2.8% YoY in the first half of 2016. What is will be the growth rate of private investment in 2016? The survey shows that, 69% of the experts expect that it would be "between 2.1 and 3.0%", 19% think that it would be "between 3.1 and 4.0%", 8% predict that it would be "2.0% or less", 3% believe that it would be "between 4.1 and 5.0%", 1% chose

"5.0% or more". In sum, more than 20% of the expert predict that the private investment growth would rise in next half of 2016.

Due to the continued decline in the private investment growth, the proportion of private investment in total investment decreased from 64.2% in 2015 to 61.5% in the first half of 2016. What are the causes? The survey shows that, 80% of the experts believe that it should be "private enterprises lack confidence in the economy". 77% think it would be the lack of effective investment objective, that is, weak macro economy environment combined with the shrink of traditional manufacturing and falling profits cause less profitable effective investment objective. 66% of the experts hold the view that new financing problems and some policy-relevant factors resulted in a situation that bank loans has largely been channeled to state-owned enterprises or back into the financial system, thus reduced private investment. Along with some default on debt, private firms are facing more and more financing challenges. 59% claimed that the tertiary industry is still being controlled, the investment fields are restricted and the approval procedure for private investment is cumbersome, thus economic policies may never be fully implemented. 36% of experts believed that the rising house prices limited the development of real economy and reduced private investment. Furthermore, other policies were put forward by 5% of experts: the orientation of private firms were ambiguous, the policies encourage private investment used to be short-term policies which cannot increase the confidence of investors among people, the macro-economic stability wasn't enough and large potential risk still exist, domestic investment environment was deteriorated and the capital outflows were increased, the monopoly power of state-owned firms reduced private investment, and the National Bureau of Statistic adjusted the data, etc.

According to the report released by NBS on July 15, 2016. China have made progress in cutting overcapacity. In the first half of 2016, the coal production declined by 9.7%, and the crude steel production decreased by 1.1%. What about the effects of curbing excess capacity? The survey shows that, 60% of the experts hold the view that the process was slow and it may affect supply-side structural reforms, 19% chose "progressed well" and 8% claimed that the process was too slow to hasten and excess capacity need to be solved as soon as possible. But 7% of the experts thought that the processes need to be slow down and adjusted slightly. 6% believed that it should be "too fast, caution". In sum, nearly 70% of the experts maintained that the process of dissolving excess capacity in the industrial sector was slow and might affect supply-side structural reforms in China.

China's total retail sales of consumer goods in 2016 were 15.61 trillion yuan, up by 10.3% YoY. What is the growth rate of China's total retail sales of consumer goods in 2016? The survey shows, that 57% of the experts expect that the total retail sales of consumer goods would increase year on year at the rate "between 10.3 and 10.8%", 34% predict that it would increase at the rate "between 9.7 and 10.2%", 5% of experts claim that it would be "between 10.9 and 11.4%", 2%

consider that it would be "11.5% or more", and 2% maintain that it would be "less than 9.6%". In sum, more than 60% of the experts predict that the growth of the total retail sales of consumer goods would continue going up in 2016.

China's total value of exports in dollar terms dropped by 7.7% in the first half of 2016 down by 8.6 percentage points over the same period last year. What is the growth rate of total value of exports in 2016? The survey shows that, 33% of the experts expect that it would be "between −2.5 and −2.1%", 33% predict that it would be "between −2.0 and −1.0%", 19% forecast that it would be "between −2.9 and −2.5%", 9% expect that it would be "less than −3.0%", and 6% forecast that it would be "between −0.9 and −0.0%". In sum, 60% of the experts predict that the exports growth would continue to decline in 2016,and nearly 40% expect that it would continue slightly rising in 2016.

3. **China's macroeconomic policies to be implemented**

By the end of 2016, China's broad money supply (M2) was 149.05 trillion yuan, grew by 11.8% YoY. What is the growth rate of China's M2 in 2016? The survey shows that, 45% of the experts predict that it would be "between 12.1 and 12.5%". 39% expect that it would be "between 11.0 and 12.0%". 11% forecast that it would be "between 12.6 and 13.0%", 5% anticipate that it would be "between 13.1 and 14.0%". In sum, the results reflect that nearly 60% of experts thought that the growth rate of M2 would rise in the second half of 2016, suggesting that China's central bank would continue to implement a moderately loose monetary policy.

China's new loans were 7.53 trillion yuan in the first half of 2016, up by 967.1 billion yuan over the same period last year. What are the roles of the new loans? The survey shows that, 75% of the experts maintain that they have helped solve the financing problems of private investment. 75% think that they have stimulated the real estate market. 57% considers that they have guaranteed the investment in infrastructure, 53% hold the view that they have not entered into the real economy, so the investment growth continues slowing down. 50% claim that these new loans have accelerated the investment growth of SOEs, and 48% believe that credit expansion has been stalled by monetary policy transmission channel. In addition, 1% of the experts put forward other views such as the loan figures can't reflect the fact because rolling over old debts with new borrowing is common among cities.

China expanded its reform to replace business tax with VAT since May 1, 2016. What is the impact of this policy have on the economy? The survey shows that, 65% of the experts expected that this policy would reduce taxes and motivate businesses to innovate, thus promote the upgrading of economy, 60% of them believed that it would promote the development of production service industry, accelerate the division of industry, elongate the industrial chain and further drives the innovation and upgrade of manufacturing enterprises. 59% claimed that it reduced national revenues due to the fact that the growth rate of national revenues fell to 1.7% in June, which was the slowest rate in 2016. 41% of the expert thought that fully implement the policy to replacing business tax with vat would reduce the financing costs of business entity and improve economic efficiency of the whole industry. Furthermore, other policies were put forward by 6% of experts: no obvious effects, it is conductive to solve parts of employment issues and guide labor in informal sectors transfer to formal sectors, firms are facing greater pressure due to the fact that nominal business tax in many industries decreased but actual tax increased, no obvious effect on tax reduction, the share of taxes of the nation increased but the taxes for business did not decrease, it is beneficial to foreign company, etc.

By the end of May in 2016, the asset-liability ratio of China's industrial enterprises above designated size is 56.8%. And according to the Bank for International Settlement (BIS), China's non-financial corporate debt was about 150% of GDP at the end of 2015. Since deleveraging is also in the context of the current supply side reform, and then, how can we reduce the high corporate debt load? The survey shows that, 81% of the experts believe that it would be the joint effort of fiscal policy and monetary policy to protecting the macro-environment of deleveraging. Reducing taxes, improving investment efficiency and creating fair competition environment along with promoting PPP to attract private investment are necessary method to enhance firm's capacity of deleveraging. 65% claim that it would be good to develop multilevel capital markets, accelerate the development of financing tools, and attract self-owned capital into stock market. 64% of them believed that we should deepen enterprise's reform along with deleveraging, such as promoting the employee stock ownership or enforcing debt-to-equity swap. Government should reduce the cost and taxes in creating a better environment, break the soft budget constraints as well as rigid payment. 60% of them maintain that debt restructuring should be promoted under the principle of market and institutionalization. 41% of the experts expect that it should improve supply-side structural reforms, raise the capability of the enterprise for sustainable development by stimulating innovation and improving social security system. In addition, other suggestions were put forward by 7% of experts: improve the enterprise system and reduce operating costs; improve the investment system and make the enterprises take responsibilities for their decisions; implement the structural tax policy, that is, raise the tax on the financial income but reduce the tax on the income of entity enterprises; make reform of political system and improve the efficiency of government; renew the management ideas and methods; absorb financial funds, especially those from first to high net-worth clients, to restructure corporate debt, and allow there funds to investment in such long-term capital instruments as preferred stocks, subprime product, and convertible debt; facilitate failure of zombie companies; etc.

4. **Projected China's average economic growth rates in 2016–20**

As to China's projected average economic growth rates during the 13th Five Year Plan (2016–20), the survey shows that 41% of the experts expected that it would be "between 6.3 and 6.5%". 39% forecast that it would be "between 6.6 and 6.8%". 14% predict that it would be "between 6.0 and 6.2%", and 6% anticipate that it would be "between 6.9 and 7.0%". In sum, most of the experts predict that China's economic would continue to slow down during the 13th Five Year Plan.

Table A.1 Forecast of major indicators of China's Economy by the CQMM team and the experts

Major indicators	By CQMM team (%)	By experts	
		Interval (%)	Ratio
GDP growth rate	6.63	6.5–6.7	59
CPI growth rate	2.01	2.1–2.5	61
PPI growth rate	−3.19	−3.8 to −2.8	67
Total retail sales of consumer goods	10.3	10.3–10.8	57
		9.7–10.2	34
Investments in fixed assets	8.97	8.1–9.0	50
		9.1 to 10.0	40
Exports in dollar terms	−6.01	−2.0 to −1.0	33
		−2.5 to −2.1	33

MIX
Papier | Fördert gute Waldnutzung
FSC® C083411

Kolibri 360 GmbH
Ferdinand-Jühlke-Straße 7
99095 Erfurt, Deutschland
produktsicherheit@kolibri360.de